P9-CDD-650

The
Princeton
Review®

READING SMART

2nd Edition

The Staff of The Princeton Review

PrincetonReview.com

Penguin
Random
House

The Princeton Review
24 Prime Parkway, Suite 201
Natick, MA 01760
E-mail: editorialsupport@review.com

Copyright © 2016 by TPR Education IP
Holdings, LLC. All rights reserved.

Published in the United States by Penguin
Random House LLC, New York, and in Canada
by Random House of Canada, a division of
Penguin Random House Ltd., Toronto.

Terms of Service: The Princeton Review Online
Companion Tools ("Student Tools") for retail
books are available for only the two most recent
editions of that book. Student Tools may be
activated only twice per eligible book purchased
for two consecutive 12-month periods, for a
total of 24 months of access. Activation of
Student Tools more than twice per book is in
direct violation of these Terms of Service and
may result in discontinuation of access to
Student Tools Services.

ISBN: 978-1-101-88227-6
eBook ISBN: 978-1-101-88228-3
ISSN: 2471-7770

The Princeton Review is not affiliated with
Princeton University.

Editor: Colleen Day
Production Editor: Liz Rutzel
Production Artist: Deborah A. Silvestrini

10 9 8 7 6 5 4 3 2 1

2nd Edition

Editorial

Rob Franek, Senior VP, Publisher
Casey Cornelius, VP Content Development
Mary Beth Garrick, Director of Production
Selena Coppock, Managing Editor
Meave Shelton, Senior Editor
Colleen Day, Editor
Sarah Litt, Editor
Aaron Riccio, Editor
Orion McBean, Editorial Assistant

Penguin Random House Publishing Team

Tom Russell, VP, Publisher
Alison Stoltzfus, Publishing Director
Jake Eldred, Associate Managing Editor
Ellen Reed, Production Manager
Suzanne Lee, Designer

Acknowledgments

I would like to thank my partners in life, Varsenik Papazian and Sylvia Papazian Krupp, for their love, support, and humor. Our holt is a regular source of sustenance. Thanks as well to my colleagues, Jonathan Chiu and Colleen Day, for the constant good they do to improve the reading skills of young (and not only young) people.

—Dr. Anthony Krupp

The Princeton Review would like to thank Jonathan Chiu and Anthony Krupp for all of their work, dedication, and fantastic updates to this edition.

Contents

Register You[r]

1 Go to **PrincetonReview.com/cracking**

2 You'll see a welcome page where you can register your book using the following ISBN: 9781101882276

3 After placing this free order, you'll either be asked to log in or to answer a few simple questions in order to set up a new Princeton Review account.

4 Finally, click on the "Student Tools" tab located at the top of the screen. It may take an hour or two for your registration to go through, but after that, you're good to go.

If you are experiencing book problems (potential content errors), please contact EditorialSupport@review.com with the full title of the book, its ISBN number (located above), and the page number of the error. Experiencing technical issues? Please e-mail TPRStudentTech@review.com with the following information:

- your full name
- e-mail address used to register the book
- full book title and ISBN
- your computer OS (Mac or PC) and Internet browser (Firefox, Safari, Chrome, etc.)
- description of technical issue

Once you've registered, you can...

- Access and download additional reading drills and corresponding answer keys

- Find printable versions of the end-of-chapter summaries

- Check to see if there have been any corrections or updates to this edition

Offline Resources

- *Grammar Smart*

- *Word Smart*

- *More Word Smart*

The
Princeton
Review®

Introduction

Why Reading?

Like it or not, reading is an essential part of everyday life, from the classroom to the workplace and everything in between. The ability to read well—that is, to read a piece of writing and understand it, as well as to retain its most important parts—is a crucial skill whether you're taking the SAT, ACT, GRE, or some other standardized test; trying to decipher a wordy email filled with technical language and jargon; or just browsing the Internet or newspaper. After all, in today's digital age, we are inundated with information on a daily basis; the ability to sift through that information and distinguish between fact and opinion, between key ideas and minor details, is an invaluable tool.

But not everyone likes to read. You may be one of those people, which is why you picked up this book. Trust us, we get it. In some situations, reading is a stressful, even overwhelming, activity, such as when you're rushing to read an entire novel the night before an important test or assignment is due. (We don't recommend that.) Reading can also be time-consuming and frequently tedious, particularly if you're reading a textbook or article that's chock full of technical jargon and terminology. Moreover, reading is more often associated with academics than with leisure; some students see reading as the one thing standing between them and a perfect test score or GPA. Because of factors like these, many people decide that they don't like reading or aren't "good at" it. But it isn't that simple.

People aren't born "good readers" or "bad readers." Rather, people who read well apply specific techniques that allow them to get the most out of what they read. However, they often do so instinctively and automatically, so they probably wouldn't be able to explain exactly what it is they do. This is where we, The Princeton Review, come in. In this book, we break down the most useful and effective reading skills and strategies and explain them in a straightforward, clear way. By the time you're done working through this book, you'll be able to approach the act of reading with confidence.

Reading Faster

Many people believe that "reading fast" and "reading well" are synonyms. We understand this assumption. After all, there are several situations—such as a timed standardized test or classroom exam, for example—in which reading speed is useful and even desirable. But speed is *not* the sole mark of a smart reader, and you shouldn't feel pressure to read quickly right away. As you work through this book, learn the strategies first; focus on comprehending passages and discerning the most important information they contain. Once you can apply the techniques, your reading speed will improve naturally, without you having to force it.

Reading Smarter

Perhaps the first test of your reading skills will be with this book. So how should you read it? First, as we just mentioned, don't try to get through every chapter as quickly as you can. Like anything, learning to read more efficiently is a process, so it's best not to rush it. Second, be an *active* reader. In other words, try to stay engaged as you read. Eliminate distractions (more on this later) to keep your attention on the task at hand. If you find yourself drifting off, or if you're memorizing rules without truly understanding them, or if you're totally confused by the exercises, stop reading. Put the book down, take a break, and then come back later. Trust us: taking a break is often just what you need to refuel your mind and find your focus again.

This book contains thirteen chapters and is divided into three parts: (1) Reading in General, (2) Reading Specific Text Types, and (3) More Reading Practice. The first part of the book discusses overall reading strategies and provides general reading comprehension practice. The second part of the book introduces you to specific types of texts and genres, explaining how to shift your strategy depending on what it is you're reading. As you might have already guessed, how you read a textbook is different from how you read a piece of literature such as a play or poem. If you're a student taking a standardized test in the near future, you may find this part of the book most helpful for test-prep purposes. Standardized tests often contain a variety of passages, and this part of the book will acquaint you with a wide range of genres and the techniques you should use when reading them.

Finally, the last part of the book contains additional reading practice, or what we call "Reading Zones." The passages and accompanying multiple-choice questions in this section cover a wide range of text types and test your understanding and verbal reasoning abilities. (The answers to these activities, as well as those in Chapters 1–12, can be found in the Appendix at the end of the book.) If you wish to extend your practice—and we encourage you to do so!—you can find additional drills online in your Student Tools. Check out the Register Your Book Online! page at the beginning of this book for instructions on accessing this online content.

Some of the techniques described in this book may be unfamiliar to you, and some may even seem strange at first. But give them a chance—they really do work. However, they require work from *you*. Don't try a technique once and then give up if it doesn't seem to help on the first shot. Trying something new, whether reading-related or not, can feel difficult and awkward at first. Accept this feeling, and remind yourself that it will pass. Strategies take practice, and using them over and over again is the only way to hone them and make them serve you. Do all of the Exercises and Reading Zones in each chapter—they are designed to help you approach reading in a specific way. The Exercises generally follow the explanation of a technique, so you can use them to gauge how well you understand the techniques and determine which strategies you need to focus on. The Reading Zones provide opportunities for you to apply the skills covered in a chapter to a passage. The passages in this book are not unlike the ones you might find on a standardized test, and may be an excerpt from a novel, a newspaper article, or an academic text. Use these Reading Zones to enrich your reading comprehension practice and experience with all different types of texts.

While we'll be teaching you specific techniques, we don't want you to obsess over the details. For example, when you first learned that electrical sockets were dangerous, did you memorize a list of rules regarding what not to do to electrical sockets? No; you understood the general idea, and when you encountered a socket, you used logic and common sense to decide what to do or not to do. You should do the same with reading. We'll explain a strategy and the general idea behind it, and you'll apply that strategy while using your common sense to decide whether a certain technique is appropriate.

Getting Started

Now comes the part where you dive into this book—but first, a word of advice. Remember that change will not happen overnight. You're not going to read this book in one sitting and wake up tomorrow as a better reader. You can, however, expect improvement over time. The more effort you put in to learning these strategies, and the more confidence you have in these techniques and yourself, the more you will grow as a reader. Also remember that your practice cannot begin and end with this book. Rather, think of this book as your personal trainer: Like a trainer, we can give you the skills and concepts, but you need to continue exercising on your own to reap the rewards. So apply what you learn here to everything you read, from school textbooks to paperwork for your job, and from novels to Twitter or blogs. Regular real-world practice will help make these reading strategies second nature so that you won't just be a "good" reader, but a truly efficient and *smarter* one.

PART I

Reading in General

Reading Zones as No-Speeding Zones

"We can skim, or we can read it slowly; we can read every word, or we can skip long passages; we can read it in the order in which it presents itself, or we can read it in any order we please.... So our relationship with books is a profoundly, intensely, essentially democratic one."

—Philip Pullman

Becoming a Better Reader

Reading well is one of the most important skills you can have in school, in work, and in life. You are reading all of the time; you're even reading right now! Seriously—you probably have a lot of experience reading tweets, texts, emails, comments on websites, and websites themselves. This all counts as reading. You may not feel confident now with certain other types of reading, such as the kind that can get you an A in literature classes or a high score on standardized tests. Our job is to help you gain more experience reading these sorts of texts, and to explain to you what is happening when you read them well.

People who read well don't necessarily know why they read well, or what they are doing. Reading is an internal process, ingrained so deeply that people are barely aware of the act of reading. It's an automatic response, like the way you raise your hands when a snowball comes flying at your face. What we have done in this book is bring that process into the open, to make it visible for you. Once you realize that there is no genetic difference between people who read well and you—only that they unconsciously use certain approaches that work well—the sooner you can realize your potential as a reader.

Driving the Speed Limit

You know that you're supposed to drive the speed limit, right? But what does that mean? If your first thought is 65 or 70 miles per hour, you're potentially correct—if you're driving on a highway. But what about a county paved road? An urban area? A school zone? Now you're remembering, right? Depending on where you are, there are completely different speeds that are appropriate. Makes sense. It would be completely irrational to drive 65 in all of these places.

The same is true for reading: You want to read at different speeds depending on what you are reading. But your common sense might not be telling you that now, the way your common sense does tell you to drive slower when it's raining. If you use the same approach to every type of reading you have to do, then sometimes you will be right on track. But other times you will be reading too fast or too slow, missing important information, wondering why you had to read the same sentence three or four times. If you listen to your common sense, you'll never be far off from the best path. Keep your common sense with you at all times; it's your best ally against reading inefficiently. Some passages are highways, but some are school zones, and sometimes it's raining. Like driving, you often need to adjust your speed depending on what it is you're reading.

Road Test

Adjusting your speed is critical to reading smart, and it's easier than you would imagine. Read the following passages, and use the line below each to note the speed at which you would read them: fast, medium, or slow.

1. Measurements of net income for the period and of financial position at the end of the period are interrelated. Revenues result from selling goods or rendering services to customers and lead to increases in assets or decreases in liabilities. Expenses indicate the services have been used in generating revenue and result in decreases in assets or increases in liabilities. Because revenues represent increases in shareholders' equity, revenues are recorded by crediting (increasing) a shareholder's equity account for the specific type of revenue and debiting either anassets or liability account.

   _____

2. Laurie Anderson endures as the poster child for performance art, although the wry sprite with spiky hair and an electric violin prefers the term "multimedia artist." The writer-composer-film-maker-performer's current output attests to her knack for slipping through borders even as she remains an avant-garde brand name.

   _____

3. Herb's house is on curvy little Glacier way, a hundred yards from Walled Lake itself and not far from the amusement park that operates summers only. I came here long ago, when I was in college, to a dense festering old dance hall called the Walled Lake Casino. It was at the time when line dances were popular in Michigan, and my two friends and I drove over from Ann Arbor, though of course we knew no one for forty miles and ended up standing against the firred, scarred old walls being wry and sarcastic about everyone. Since then, Mr. Smallwood has informed me, the Casino has burned down.

These three passages are different in tone, style, vocabulary, and pace. Each one has ways into it, and how much you get out of the passage depends on you identifying the best way to read it. The main idea is that writers writing on different topics use different approaches to get their point across. If you read the first and third passages at the same speed, you're going to miss a lot from both.

Identifying what you are reading and why you are reading it is the first step in becoming a smarter reader. Let's look at the passages one by one and see what clues each passage has as to how you should read it.

Passage 1: Textbook Reading

If you made it through without falling asleep, and if you were able to decipher the academic prose, give yourself a pat on the back. Do you remember what to do to an account ledger when you sell goods? How are the measurements of net income related on the two statements? You can expect to retain very little from this passage if you don't lower your speed.

There are many tip-offs that you should read this slowly. Words are repeated in a way that can make you zone out, it is filled with specific, inaccessible, unexplained terminology, and there is no reference to anything other than itself. It is very easy to stop and find yourself lost in this kind of passage, having read words with no idea what they mean. In later chapters, we'll look at specific techniques to keep your head in the page, but for now, be concerned with pacing. You should read this passage slowly. Any time you need to learn specific facts, particularly when technical jargon is involved, slow down and learn more. If you have to read a passage three or four times to decipher it, then it's better to slow down and get it right the first or second time.

Passage 2: Journalistic Reading

The second passage reads a bit as if someone were lecturing to you. Newspapers and magazines take this informational tone. Most news stories have an opinion, and they present information in that light. This kind of passage is journalistic, and it will combine some of the academic tone of the first with the conversational tone of the third. The words are sometimes more complex than they needed to be. Notice that the phrase "attests to her knack for slipping through borders" can be rephrased as "shows that she works outside the box." You can translate the complex words into the simpler ideas if you read this passage at a moderate speed, which will allow you to identify what's going on. What is the author talking about? Does he like Anderson? What's his opinion?

Passage 3: Narrative Reading

The third passage tells a story. The retention level for most people is highest on this kind of passage. Passages with physical images, with dialogue, and with clearly identified characters and actions allow the reader to achieve a high comprehension even when reading at a faster speed. Do you remember the name of the lake? Anything they did? Fiction, narrative discourse, writing that sounds like talking or describing, is the easiest to deal with.

Planning the Trip

Once you can identify the type of passage you have to read, you should go into it with expectations. What do we mean by expectations?

Ask yourself the following questions:

- What do I need to get out of this piece?
- Do I need to memorize a bunch of facts?
- Do I just need an overview?
- Will I be tested on this stuff?
- What can I expect from a passage like this?

One thing you should notice is that your approach to reading is affected not only by the type of passage, but also by your purpose for reading it. For example, you'll read a biography of David Bowie one way on the beach and another way for a sociology class. If you are going to be tested on material, or need to master information, you are going to go slower, highlight phrases, take notes in the margin or write notes on paper, and use other techniques to reinforce comprehension. If you are going to read a paper or magazine where the information presented may or may not be useful to you, you want to use a different technique, such as increasing your pace to get the main idea, rather than focusing on memorizing all the details. You can always go back to a detail if you're going to be tested on it. All you have to know is where to find it. If you are reading a work of fiction for pleasure, you will probably read faster than in the other two situations, but not in a hurry. This is a pleasant road trip where you enjoy the journey more than memorizing all the things that pass by.

The following chart is a general guideline for deciding what pace you will need to read different types of writing. Most of all, make sure you're comfortable with that reading speed. The idea is to strike the right balance between speed and comprehension.

PACING CHART		
Type of Writing	**Requirement**	**Pace**
Textbook • English • History • Math • Science	• Memorization • Overall Mastery • Tested	Slow
Journalistic • Newspapers • Magazines • Memos • Essays	• Overall Understanding • Solid Familiarity • Important to know, but most likely never tested	Medium
Other Writing • Fiction • Personal Histories • Narrative Discourse	• Basic Understanding • Basic Familiarity • Not Tested	Fast

Remember, this list is useful as a general guideline, but it is not meant to be an absolute rule. For example, some works of fiction are dense and will require you to read more slowly; similarly, you may come across an article or piece of academic writing that you're able to get through more quickly. Use your judgment and common sense.

Exercise 1

Read the following sentences. Mark next to each how you would read the passage: Fast, Medium, or Slow. You can check your answers using the answer key on page 234.

1. There I was, way off my ambitions, getting deeper in love every minute, and all of a sudden I didn't care.

   _____

2. The reforms in Russia continue in a "herky-jerky" fashion and, therefore, so does the economic growth of the former Soviet state. The capricious attitude of the Russian leadership to questions of finance has unnerved the watching world.

   _____

3. Mary closed her eyes and saw stars exploding in brilliant flowers of light. It was the Fourth of July in her head, an orchestra of pleasure.

   _____

4. If e.e. cummings is considered a genius, then too must William Carlos Williams, for his poetry most closely approximates the shape of what cummings attempted to explore. Both took advantage of spatial constructs to open doorways to interpretive possibility.

   _____

5. Fasten the tube with the E-Bar connector, making sure to seal both ends with bonding glue, scoring the edges first to ensure a snug fit. Test for leakage by running warm water through the tube.

   _____

6. Maria poked her head from behind the door and called, "If you knew anything, you would know I can never love a person like you!" She stomped upstairs, leaving little bits of Vladimir's heart in shreds on the living room floor.

_____

7. The regression is valid for the first, second, and third tenths of the population, but once the fourth and fifth are included, the error factor (t-regression) retreats to a degree of 20%. With inconsistencies in the regression apparent, the entire study must be reconsidered.

_____

8. A person's worth cannot be judged solely by his actions; his intentions must also be taken into account. In acting rashly, my client committed a crime. In rushing to help a friend, he hurt someone else. At all times, only the possible positive effects of his action were on his mind.

_____

9. "He needs me like he needs a head cold," quipped Martin, sipping his latte. Quickly, he spit out the frothy beverage on the rug. Someone had replaced the latte with sour milk.

_____

10. The 24 vertebrae in the spinal column are divided into three parts; the cervical, the thoracic, and the lumbar, of which the first two cervical vertebrae are known as the Atlas (C-1) and the Axis (C-2).

_____

11. Did madness take over Genet in his final days, as the passion of his life had been spent? None but his lover shall ever know. His lover took the secrets of Genet's final days to the grave. Buried in a layer of mystery, Genet's ending is extended into all of our futures.

_____

12. Raising temperature is simple: First, seal off all possible manner of perspiration. This reduces the body's natural cooling efficiency by up to 80%. Then, provide the subject with large quantities of food and water. This will stimulate internal processes that cause the temperature to rise dramatically. The harder the body works, the more energy it produces.

_____

13. Elizabeth Montgomery played Samantha on the hit 1960s television show *Bewitched*. A number of actors, however, played her daughter, Tabitha. Regardless of the changing cast, the show enjoyed years of rating prosperity until Elizabeth Montgomery's retirement seven years after the show's inception.

_____

14. Darryl stood face to face with the moose. The moose pawed at the ground. Darryl lowered to a three-point-stance. The moose bellowed. Darryl yelled something about the moose's mother. The moose charged, antlers low. Darryl darted forward, using exceptional blocking technique. If he were facing a human opponent, that is.

_____

15. Up at Altamont, 1,500 windmills stand, braced against the wind. They are situated on the crests of 700 small natural inclines, and their arms pinwheel in crazy circles at up to 120 miles per hour. They form a church, of sorts; a church dedicated to the proposition that natural energies can be harnessed, and used, without destroying fossil fuels and creating pollution. Professor Jonathan Davis, who runs the institute, is the pastor at this church, and he makes it known that he will accept all comers into his fold.

Things to Take with You

Whenever you start to read for a purpose, ask yourself the following questions:

- What kind of reading is it?
- What do I need to get out of it?
- What pace should I be using?
- What techniques should I be using?

The chapters that follow will help you answer these questions.

Getting Into the Zone

To help you achieve your reading potential, we have included throughout the book a number of short passages we call Reading Zones. The Reading Zones include a variety of writing styles and forms: short stories, textbook passages, magazine articles—even a couple of poems. Some of the passages will be hard, some will be boring, some will be fun; but all of them will help you improve your reading skills.

Reading Zone 1

Start by doing what you would do on any reading exam: Read the following passage and answer the questions. You can check your answers on page 234.

Although the conventional American view has been that parties would perform better if they were internally democratic, the question is by no means as simple as the standard view suggests. Our starting point must be the functions we want parties to perform, and to perform well. If one of these is to facilitate popular control over elected officials—as it surely is—then it does not follow that this result is to be obtained only, or even best, by internal party democracy.

An analogy may help to clarify the point. Political parties are sometimes likened to business firms competing for customers—the customers being in this case the voters. And just as business firms are driven by competition to satisfy consumers, even if they are internally not governed by consumers in the way that a consumers' cooperative is, so, it is sometimes argued, competitive parties will fulfill all of the essential functions of democratic control listed earlier, even though each party is internally controlled by its leaders. If the main function of competing parties is to ensure that the views of voters are translated into government policies, then it is less important that parties be internally democratic than they be responsive to the view of the voters.

Would greater internal democracy ensure that the parties would be more responsive to the voters? If we take presidential nominations as the most crucial test case, the answer is not as clear as one might hope. For one thing, changes in procedures intended to ensure greater internal democracy may only shift control from one set of political activists to another. Political activists are, roughly speaking, of two kinds. One is the familiar party "regular," party leaders who over a considerable period of time occupy positions of influence in the party and regularly devote a large share of their time, energy, and resources to party activities. The others are the "irregulars," insurgents and amateurs who become active in behalf of a particular cause or candidate. Having been drawn into a campaign, some of the irregulars may later become regulars, but many drop out after the campaign is over, or bide their time until another attractive cause or candidate comes along.

The difficulty is that the insurgents may be no more representative of the opinions of a majority of voters than the regulars—and quite possibly they may be less so. Both parties provide evidence on this point. In 1964, the most ideologically conservative activists in the Republican Party, a group of insurgents whose views probably represented only a minority among Republican voters and an even smaller minority in the electorate as a whole, seized control of the nominating convention from the Republican "establishment," nominated Senator Barry Goldwater and suffered one of the three or four worst defeats in the entire history of the party.

The Goldwater insurgency in the Republican Party was duplicated in the Democratic Party by the nomination of George McGovern in 1972. McGovern was an insurgent candidate who gathered around him an enthusiastic core of activists, most of whom were irregulars without prior political experience, and his candidacy was probably aided somewhat—though not decisively—by a change in party rules intended to make the Democratic Convention more representative of previously underrepresented groups—specifically blacks, women, and youth. The McGovern forces won a majority of delegates elected in the primaries and then went on to victory in the Democratic Convention. In the election, McGovern suffered the worst defeat of any Democratic candidate in fifty years.

The delegates to the Democratic Convention, it turned out, were highly unrepresentative of Democratic supporters. Of all the groups at the convention, the insurgent McGovern delegates deviated most from the views of rank-and-file Democrats. The women delegates chosen under the new rules were not at all representative of rank-and-file Democratic women, nor the youth of rank-and-file young people. Even the black delegates were rather unrepresentative of attitudes among the black population at large and among black Democratic supporters.

Ironically, in 1972, the delegates to the Republican Convention were much closer to the views of rank-and-file Democrats in the country at large than were the delegates to the Democratic Convention. In the face of experiences like these, some people concluded that the parties were still not democratic enough in their internal organization since in both cases the insurgents proved to be unrepresentative of broader opinion. It was thought necessary to bring about even more control by rank-and-file party followers, reducing even further the influence of party leaders and activists. From this perspective, the rapidly expanding participation in presidential primaries noted above is a sign of health in the political parties.

1. According to the passage, what does "internally democratic" mean?
   (A) Only Democrats are members.
   (B) Both Democrats and Republicans can be members.
   (C) The organization obeys the wishes of all people.
   (D) The election of delegates is done democratically.
   (E) The organization was founded by Democrats.

2. The main point of the passage is to
   - (A) show the health and the internal voting process of the Republican Party in the 1960s and 1970s
   - (B) show the abundance of internal democracy in the two-party system
   - (C) illuminate the internal voting process
   - (D) show that internal democracy does not necessarily ensure accurate representation
   - (E) show the health of the Democratic Party

3. Barry Goldwater's defeat can be ascribed to
   - (A) a small but vocal minority within the Democratic Party
   - (B) competition from George McGovern
   - (C) excessive conservatism among mainstream Republicans
   - (D) the inexperience of his party's "regulars"
   - (E) the capture of the Republican platform by extremists

4. Which statement would the author most likely agree with?
   - (A) Political parties are run like businesses.
   - (B) Political parties should be run like businesses.
   - (C) Businesses should be run more democratically.
   - (D) Political parties can be likened to businesses in their organization.
   - (E) Business and politics don't mix.

5. According to the passage, a sign of health in the political parties is
   - (A) the expanding participation in presidential primaries
   - (B) the expanding membership of both major political parties
   - (C) the declining number of rule changes since 1974
   - (D) the declining number of party "irregulars" in both major political parties
   - (E) the expanding participation in the presidential elections

Reflection

For any question you got wrong, go back and leave notes next to each answer choice indicating why it is correct or incorrect. It's important that you not only practice, but also reflect on your performance! This way, you'll see what issues give you trouble and gain a better understanding of how to improve.

Chapter 1 Summary

- Adjust your reading speed and overall approach depending on what it is you're reading.

- Academic texts, such as a textbook or manual, should be read more slowly in order for you to absorb all of the information. On the other hand, articles and literature with a conversational tone can be read more quickly. Use your common sense to determine how quickly you can read while retaining the content of a text.

- Set expectations before you read something. In other words, identify what it is that you want to get out of it. This will help you determine your reading pace.

- Before you begin reading, ask yourself questions such as

    o What kind of reading is it?

    o What do I need to get out of it?

    o What pace should I be using?

    o What techniques should I be using?

CHAPTER 2

Reading Is Physical

> "We often think of reading as a cerebral activity concerned with the abstract—with thoughts and ideas, tone and themes, metaphors and motifs. As far as our brains are concerned, however, text is a tangible part of the physical world we inhabit."
>
> —Ferris Jabr

On the next sunny day, go to your local park and look for people who seem to be reading a book. (It may be on a tablet, we know.) Observe their behaviors: They recline, holding a book in one hand, occasionally putting the book down or looking around at the other people. Later, they will remember the day as pleasant, the people as relaxed, and probably not much about the book they brought. Completely relaxed approaches and environments just don't lead to high levels of reading retention. So if your friends tell you that listening to music on your comfortable couch with the television remote and your cell phone next to you is the best way to read, don't listen to them. That is, if reading smarter is your goal.

On the other hand, sitting in a perfectly silent room with flickering fluorescent lights while a dozen people furiously scribble notes and tear out their hair is not any better. At best, you will read at the same levels of speed and retention as before and give yourself a headache.

Where, then, is a person to read efficiently?

Find the Right Place

Find a place both comfortable and quiet, with few distractions and little noise. This is not always possible, but if you can find such a spot, your reading efficiency (particularly your comprehension) can improve dramatically. Choose a place where the lighting is bright but not overly so. Indirect lighting is best. Your eyes are the workhorse of reading, and treating them poorly is the surest way to give yourself eyestrain, headaches, and a good excuse to stop reading. Do not have distractions available. A nearby phone, a TV, or a video game can all call to you, saying "Don't read—I need some attention!" and drag you away from the task at hand.

You will do this: Turn your phone off or put it on silent. Then put it away somewhere so that you can't see it. We know it's hard; we can empathize. But as Shia LaBeouf would say: Just do it.

If you have music playing, choose music with no words. Even if you think you concentrate well with all music, trust us: The words in the lyrics tend to seep into your consciousness and mix with the words you are reading. There's a very small part of the brain (called Wernicke's area) that processes all of the words you read and hear, and it doesn't do well at multitasking. But don't believe the people who tell you that "classical music" is best. The only part of that statement that is kind of true is that *instrumental* music is best. A lot of "classical" music is instrumental, but so is a lot of jazz, as well as contemporary dance music. Even Mozart composed pieces with lyrics, and we strongly advise you not to listen to them while you're reading. (Don't believe us? Google "Queen of the Night Aria" right now and listen to it as you read the rest of this chapter. Let us know when you give up.) Therefore, let your Wernicke's area focus on reading, and the other parts of your brain can be happily stimulated by music without words.

If you cannot find the perfect place to read, don't despair. Reading can be done anywhere—but you have to increase the intensity of your concentration in proportion to the number of distractions around you. A student once failed a European history exam because she was living in a house with a nest of wasps outside the window. She would sit down to read the textbook, but every time she would feel a light tickle of wind on her neck, she would jerk around, looking for the wasp that was about to sting her. Her concentration was so divided that when the exam question was "What was the effect of growing European fractionism?" she could only remember how European fractionism made her nervous and anxious, and reminded her of wasps. Her professor was not very sympathetic.

You will find that as you begin to read smarter, your concentration will improve, and all of this location scouting will be less necessary. But for now, do think about physical realities and choose a reading location with few distractions. If you were running in a race, you wouldn't want to have to weave through a crowd of people to get to the finish line. Any one of them could knock you down and out of the race. If you have the opportunity, give yourself the best chance of success.

Let's Get Physical

Look at a group of excellent students in the moments before they take an essay test. You should see alert, focused people who, the minute the exam begins, open their test booklets and scan the pages deftly for the important information. They are rapidly and efficiently trying to derive the primary questions from their test books.

Look at how these students physically engage themselves in the test: They are slightly hunched over the reading, completely engrossed. They have a pen or pencil in one hand, and with the other hand, they may be pointing to the words or paragraphs on the page as they read. They become physically involved with their reading—and you should too.

We're not asking you to recreate testing situations—no one needs (or deserves) that much stress in her life. But you should become physically involved with your reading. If your posture is poor, and your back begins to hurt after ten minutes of reading, your speed, comprehension, and stamina will all suffer. If you sit back and wait for whatever it is you're reading to grab you, you've already lost. No matter how engrossing or difficult any reading is, the most effective reading comes from involving yourself in the subject.

Be aggressive with your approach to reading, both mentally and physically. If you are intimidated by a book, you're going to have a struggle on your hands, and in the end the book always wins. If you walk away, leave the book on a table, join the French Foreign Legion, travel the world, win a Nobel Peace Prize, that's all great. But when you come back to the book, you will still feel the same way about it. The situation is not going to spontaneously change. This means that *you* have to change.

Now What?

Now that you've found your comfortable—but not too comfortable—well-lit spot. You have your music without words playing. You have a pen or pencil, and your phone is put away (on silent, and you cannot see it). You're ready to read, and you open the book. Then, you start to read and...nothing changes. It still takes you a long time to get through a few pages, and you don't recall many of the ideas or details. Instead of being in the zone, you are zoning out.

A journey of a thousand miles begins with a single step, and you've just learned how to tie your shoes. So let's talk about the mechanics of reading: how anyone, from the slowest to the fastest of readers, actually reads. Much of the technical stuff is not necessary for you to become a smarter reader, but it helps you understand why you may not be reading as effectively as you could be.

The Eyes Don't Understand (But the Brain Does)

How does a person read? It starts with sensations, usually visual sensations. (Reading Braille also starts with sensations: in this case, with tactile sensations as the finger moves across the page.) Although you may think that your eyes travel smoothly across the page, they don't. They jerk across the page, grabbing clumps of information and sending them to your brain. Your eyes don't do any actual reading (or understanding)—this takes place in your brain.

So what goes on in your head while you read? Your brain takes these clusters of information and sorts through them, looking for patterns that it recognizes. These patterns include features, letters, words, phrases, clauses, and paragraphs. Your brain assembles all of these groups into coherent thoughts, and you perceive the meaning. That's what reading feels like. Of course, all this stuff happens simultaneously—your eyes are grabbing clusters and sending them to your brain while one part of your brain is sorting and another is assembling.

Two possibilities might occur to you now: (1) The faster you can train your eye to take in these clusters, the faster you can read. Although there are books and courses that will promise to teach you "speed reading," we find that this strategy is not a fruitful way to go. The other idea is that (2) the more efficiently you can train your brain to recognize these patterns, the more rapidly and effectively you can read. We are all for brain training; the rest of this book focuses on this idea.

Reading with Your Hands

Can you remember how you read when you were in elementary school? There was probably a phase in which you used your hands or your finger to keep your place as you read. Somewhere along the way, you probably lost this habit, but we want to encourage you to get hands-on with your reading again. You might want to point to a part of the text with one finger while you also look at a question and answer choices: This is a great way to keep focus and not lose your place. You may also want to "bracket" part of the text with your thumb and pointer finger, so that you can keep your focus on a given paragraph or chunk of text.

There is nothing childish about this. We human beings are a tool-using species, and it is totally rational that you would want to use tools like your hands to help you make sense of things. As you read the following passage and then answer questions about it, make a point of getting physically hands-on with the text!

Reading Zone 2

Read the following passage and answer the questions. You can find the answers on page 235.

On Tuesday, May 22, 1980, a man named Henry Hill did what seemed to him the only sensible thing to do: He decided to cease to exist. He was in the Nassau County jail, facing a life sentence in a massive narcotics conspiracy. The federal prosecutors were asking him about his role in the $6 million Lufthansa German Airlines robbery, the largest successful cash robbery in American history. The New York City police were in line behind the feds to ask him about the ten murders that followed the Lufthansa heist. The Justice Department wanted to talk to him about his connection with a murder that also involved Michele Sindona, the convicted Italian financier. The Organized Crime Strike Force wanted to know about the Boston College basketball players he had bribed in a point-shaving scheme. Treasury agents were looking for the crates of automatic weapons and Claymore mines he had stolen from a Connecticut armory. The Brooklyn district attorney's office wanted information about a body they had found in a refrigeration truck, which was frozen so stiff it needed two days to thaw before the medical examiner could perform an autopsy.

When Henry Hill had been arrested only three weeks earlier, it hadn't been big news. There were no front-page stories in the newspapers and no segments on the evening news. His arrest was just another of dozens of the slightly exaggerated multimillion-dollar drug busts that police make annually in their search for paragraphs of praise. But the arrest of Henry Hill was a prize beyond measure. Hill had grown up in the mob. He was only a mechanic, but he knew everything. He knew how it worked. He knew who oiled the machinery. He knew, literally, where the bodies were buried. If he talked, the police knew that Henry Hill could give them the key to dozens of indictments and convictions. And even if he didn't talk, Henry Hill knew that his own friends would kill him just as they had killed nearly everyone who had been involved in the Lufthansa robbery. In jail Henry heard the news: His own protector, Paul Vario, the seventy-year-old mob chief in whose house Henry had been raised from childhood, was through with him; and James "Jimmy the Gent" Burke, Henry's closest friend, his confidant and partner, the man he had been scheming and hustling with since he was thirteen years old, was planning to murder him.

Under the circumstances, Henry made his decision: He became part of the Justice Department's Federal Witness Protection Program. His wife, Karen, and their children, Judy, fifteen, and Ruth, twelve, ceased to exist along with him. They were give new identities. It should be said that it was slightly easier for Henry Hill to cease to exist than it might have been for the average citizen, since the actual evidence of Hill's existence was extraordinarily slim. His home was apparently owned by his mother-in-law. His car was registered in his wife's name. His Social Security cards and driver's licenses—he had several of each—were forged and made out of fictitious names. He had never voted and never paid taxes. He had never even flown on an airplane using a ticket made out in his own name. In fact, one of the only pieces of documentary evidence that proved without doubt that Henry Hill had lived—besides his birth certificate—was his yellow sheet, the police record of arrests he had begun as a teenage apprentice to the mob.

1. According to the passage, Henry Hill's arrest was described by police as
   (A) slightly exaggerated
   (B) big news
   (C) just another drug bust
   (D) a "prize beyond measure"
   (E) the beginning of the end for the Mafia in the United States

2. Why was Hill's arrest so important?
   - (A) Hill's friends and colleagues were scheming to kill him.
   - (B) He had deep-frozen a body.
   - (C) It allowed him to join the Witness Protection Program.
   - (D) He had information on many unsolved crimes.
   - (E) He was the head of a major organized crime empire.

3. Why was it so easy for Hill to "disappear"?
   - (A) His mother-in-law bought his house.
   - (B) There was little legal evidence of his existence.
   - (C) His family came with him.
   - (D) He had a long "yellow sheet."
   - (E) He had many underworld contacts.

4. Which best describes Hill's position in the mob?
   - (A) Powerful and knowledgeable
   - (B) Low but powerful
   - (C) Low but knowledgeable
   - (D) High and knowledgeable
   - (E) A relative of Paul Vario

5. According to the passage, Paul Vario
   - (A) was murdered by Henry Hill
   - (B) had ten people murdered following the Lufthansa crime
   - (C) raised Henry Hill
   - (D) knew Henry from the age of thirteen
   - (E) headed an international crime family

Reflection

For any question you got wrong, go back and leave notes next to each answer choice indicating why it is correct or incorrect. It's important that you not only practice, but also reflect on your performance! This way, you'll see what issues give you trouble and gain a better understanding of how to improve.

Chapter 2 Summary

- Choosing the right reading environment is key. Find a place that is quiet and free of distractions.

- Set yourself up for success by making sure that your environment's conditions are conducive to reading and staying focused. For example, the lighting should be bright enough, and all technology—smart phones, smart watches, or tablets, for example—should be out reach.

- If you like to listen to music while reading, your best bet is instrumental music (music without lyrics).

- Become physically engaged with your reading. Highlight, underline, take notes, or point to the words on the page to keep your focus as you read.

Why Are You Reading That?

"I think we ought to read only the kind of books that wound or stab us. If the book we're reading doesn't wake us up with a blow to the head, what are we reading for? ... A book must be the axe for the frozen sea within us."

—Franz Kafka

Conquering Different Text Types

So you're ready to be aggressive, to attack your reading, and to approach it smartly, smoothly, and with no reservations. Great! What next? Are you just going to dive into any different type of reading with one approach? Would you read a physics textbook the same way you would *The Hunger Games*, or a book of poetry the same way you would a news article? Such an approach could lead you back to reading the way you did before, which is why you need to tailor your reading strategy to the type of text you're reading. But how do you go about doing this?

Identify Why

You must identify the type of reading you are about to undertake. In the first chapter, we talked about three different types of reading you may encounter. These are large, inclusive groups that are meant to serve as general guidelines (which will be repeated in this chapter). The most important questions about your reading will be addressed here. And before you start reading, you should have these questions answered somewhere in your mind.

The first question you must ask yourself before you sit down to read something is: Why am I reading this? "Because I have to" is not a useful response. Unless you know what you need to get out of your reading, you are not ready to begin reading yet.

Why Identify Why?

Why you read something is as important as *what* you are reading. If you won a ten-minute shopping spree in a supermarket, you wouldn't just take one of everything, or only get forty bags of dog food. You would tailor your shopping to the things you need. You would make a plan to use those ten minutes to your greatest advantage. Identifying *Why* tells you how you need to approach the reading, as well as how to tailor your approach so that you can get what you need.

Whether you're a student, professional, or casual reader, you cannot afford to begin reading without first knowing what you need to get out of it.

Ask yourself the following questions before you begin reading:

---

1. **What degree of knowledge do I need to take from this information: Intimate, Casual, or Passing? Or to put it another way: Final, Test, or Quiz?**

2. **What type of reading is it: Fast, Medium, or Slow?**

3. **How long will I need this knowledge: Until Tomorrow, For a Long Time, or For Life?**

After you have answered these questions, you will be in a better position to "read smart." But *how* do you answer these questions? Let's look at them one by one.

What Degree of Knowledge Do I Need to Take from This Information?

Ask yourself why you are reading the material. Is it an assignment? Will you be tested on the contents? Do you need it for work? Will you use it every day? Or is it just a secondary piece of information you will need every now and then? Or is it a magazine or a blog, where you enjoy the articles but are not sure you will ever need to know the details? The speed at which you want to read these pieces depends mainly on your answers to these questions.

What Type of Reading Is It?

Is it a casual, chatty text with lots of dialogue and action that you can just whip through? Or is it a series of symbols and graphs, explaining a very esoteric concept? Is this an argument or a presentation? (This is kind of a trick question—nearly all good writing is an argument of some kind). By answering this question, you can decide on an appropriate reading speed and focus.

How Long Will I Need This Knowledge?

If you are reading a book on how to hypnotize people into doing your absolute bidding, you'll want to remember that for the rest of your life. If you are reading the menu in a restaurant you may never visit again, you are not going to want to memorize part of the menu in case you are quizzed on it five minutes after you order. The way you do remember very important things is by restating those things in your own words. Once you remember it in your own way, it is yours forever. If you need something in the short term, you should mark the text.

Exercise 3

In the following exercise, identify how you would classify the types of reading. We've done the first one for you. You can check your answers on page 235.

1. You are reading a chapter in a physics textbook that will be on the final.

   What degree of knowledge do I need to
   take from this information?   _intimate_

   What type of reading is it?   _slow_

   How long will I need this knowledge?   _long time_

2. You pick up a magazine at the hair salon while waiting for a chair to be free.

   What degree of knowledge do I need to
   take from this information?   _____

   What type of reading is it?   _____

   How long will I need this knowledge?   _____

3. You are reading the business section of a newspaper before you go to your job as a stockbroker.

What degree of knowledge do I need to
take from this information? _____

What type of reading is it? _____

How long will I need this knowledge? _____

4. You are lying in bed, reading a novel about an English spy in World War II Germany.

What degree of knowledge do I need to
take from this information? _____

What type of reading is it? _____

How long will I need this knowledge? _____

5. You are reading a report on the environment that you requested for work.

What degree of knowledge do I need to
take from this information? _____

What type of reading is it? _____

How long will I need this knowledge? _____

6. You are reading a traffic ticket.

What degree of knowledge do I need to
take from this information? _____

What type of reading is it? _____

How long will I need this knowledge? _____

7. You are reading a police report on your cousin Willie.

What degree of knowledge do I need to
take from this information?   _____

What type of reading is it?   _____

How long will I need this knowledge?   _____

8. You are reading a math textbook to review some concepts for
your physics final.

What degree of knowledge do I need to
take from this information?   _____

What type of reading is it?   _____

How long will I need this knowledge?   _____

9. You are reading your spouse's old love letters you found at the
top of the closet.

What degree of knowledge do I need to
take from this information?   _____

What type of reading is it?   _____

How long will I need this knowledge?   _____

10. You are reading the recommendations of a prospective employee.

What degree of knowledge do I need to
take from this information?   _____

What type of reading is it?   _____

How long will I need this knowledge?   _____

11. You are reading Internet memes.

What degree of knowledge do I need to
take from this information?   _____

What type of reading is it?   _____

How long will I need this knowledge?   _____

12. You are reading *War and Peace* the night before the final exam.

What degree of knowledge do I need to
take from this information?   _____

What type of reading is it?   _____

How long will I need this knowledge?   _____

Reading Zone 3

Read the following passage and answer the questions that follow.
You can check your answers on page 236.

Sherwood Anderson in his *Memoirs* testifies to the nearly
miraculous sense of ease and liberation with which the
stories of *Winesburg, Ohio* were written—poured out in a
Chicago room in a concentrated fury of creations, sometimes two or three stories in a week. If his account of their
composition is literally true, it is a symbolic parallel to
the creative exuberance of the Twenties. The *Winesburg*
stories speak with the voice of the Twenties, too, in their
rebellion against lingering Victorianisms, middle-class
repressions, Midwestern pieties, Puritan hypocrisies,
village narrowness—all the things which hampered and
limited the "life of realization" upon which Anderson and
his whole generation were bent.

Individually the stories of *Winesburg, Ohio* do not represent Anderson's best and richest work, and we have acknowledged that fact by selecting a story from another book, *The Triumph of the Egg*. But collectively they are both impressive and of absolutely first importance. They are revolutionary in more than their disregard of conventional morals. The outraged protest that they inspired may even have been obscurely aesthetic in part, for these were no stories by conventional standards; even Anderson's friend Floyd Dell said so; Mencken said so; the reviewers said so. They were little vignettes of buried lives, throbs of muffled desire, sketches of characters foundering among the village tribalisms, glimpses of torment behind drawn (and sometimes undrawn) blinds. They were not only plotless, but they did not even make use of the sensuous impressionism by which Crane and Steele could impress by mere vividness. These stories moved obscurely, like nightthings.

To this day the warmest admirers of Anderson cannot quite say how they get their effects. The style is flat, the method more narrative than dramatic; and yet Winesburg's people have the terrible shamefaced look of people caught in something unspeakably persona. The suppressed emotions of their lives burst out of them like moans or cries, and they compel attention and exact sympathy as more cunningly made and steered characters could not. The influence of Chekhov, obviously, is strong here: Chekhov was one of the new and exciting writers of whom Anderson's mind was full, and it was not entirely unjust that a reviewer should later call him the "phallic Chekhov." It may be precisely the strong Chekhovian sympathy that makes *Winesburg, Ohio* a great book—William Faulkner says it is the only great book that Anderson ever wrote. "Unlighted Lamps" is our choice because it contains, along with the themes of frustration and loss and yearning and human waste that were the soul of *Winesburg*, the rich and warmly felt background of the county fairgrounds and race tracks where many of his best non-*Winesburg* stories are laid. If a single story is to represent Anderson, this will serve as well as any, and better than most.

And after Anderson, the deluge. Two of the major novelists of the Twenties, Dreiser and Sinclair Lewis, were never successful with the short story, but consider those who were: Fitzgerald, Hemingway, Faulkner, Katherine Anne Porter, Steele, Lardner, and, in addition, Edith Wharton and Willa Cather and Ellen Glasgow, in the twilight of their powers but still producing. On its short stories alone, the Twenties would have been notable. And supporting the great figures, packed around them like excelsior in a tight box, was an astonishingly large and astonishingly good body of lesser writers upon whose work and against whose competition the best ones grew. You do not sharpen an axe against a wheel of cheese; neither do you produce great writers without the pressure of a solid body of competing talent. It is from its secondary figures as well as from its great ones that a period gets its quality. Yet the great ones make themselves known unmistakably.

From his earliest stories—dismissed as mere contest by some of the editors to whom he sent them—Hemingway impressed those who knew him as somebody inevitably special. His first books, *Three Stories and Ten Poems* and *In Our Time* were hardly more than a sample of what was to come, and yet there was a widespread feeling that a giant was on his way up, as witness Edmund Wilson's early review in *The Dial* in October 1924. It may be, as William Faulkner has said, that Hemingway found out early what he could do, and has continued to do it, and that this constitutes a deficiency in him, a lack of daring. On the other hand, most readers will find plentiful signs of progress and growth from "Up in Michigan" and the early vignette of *In Our Time* to "The Snows of Kilimanjaro," or "The Old Man and the Sea." Incorporated in this change is evidence that Hemingway, like Chekhov and James, has increasingly chafed against the artificial constrictions of the short story, and has moved more and more toward James's "blessed nouvelle." His first stories were vignettes less than a page long; his last one, just as true a short story, his long enough to make a small book. It is a long way from the things he was producing when as a young correspondent in Paris he was learning to write, "beginning with the simplest things."

1. The primary subject of the passage can best be summarized as
   (A) short story writers of the Twenties
   (B) a book called *Winesburg, Ohio*
   (C) Sherwood Anderson and Anton Chekov
   (D) Sherwood Anderson and Ernest Hemingway
   (E) Ernest Hemingway and Anton Chekov

2. Anderson's stories could best be described as
   (A) conventional
   (B) similar to Hemingway's
   (C) revolutionary
   (D) supportive of Victorianism
   (E) intricately structured and plotted

3. According to the passage, what makes secondary writers important?
   (A) They have an axe to grind.
   (B) They make inferior writers feel more adequate.
   (C) They make primary writers look better by contrast.
   (D) The competition improves writers in general.
   (E) They supply extra packing material.

4. How do most readers feel about Hemingway's artistic progress?
   (A) His lack of daring made him just keep doing what he was good at.
   (B) "In Our Time" is better than "The Old Man and the Sea."
   (C) He eventually advocated "beginning with the simplest things."
   (D) His success was inevitable.
   (E) Over time, he began to flourish within the boundaries of the short story.

5. The "deluge" referred to in the passage means
   (A) the uncontrolled downpouring
   (B) the unstoppable flooding
   (C) the unanticipated promulgation
   (D) the rapid decrease
   (E) the overwhelming emergence

Reflection

For any question you got wrong, go back and leave notes next to each answer choice indicating why it is correct or incorrect. It's important that you not only practice, but also reflect on your performance! This way, you'll see what issues give you trouble and gain a better understanding of how to improve.

Chapter 3 Summary

- Before you begin to read:
    - Identify *why* you are reading.
    - Determine what you need to get out of what you're reading. What degree of knowledge do you need to take away about the subject at hand—intimate, casual, or passing?
    - Know your reading pace before you begin to read (fast, medium, or slow).
    - Ask yourself how long you will need to remember the information in the passage, article, novel, etc. This will also affect how you read.

CHAPTER 4

Reading Comprehension

"Only in some very special cases is comprehension the point of reading—in things like recipes and 'reading material.' The point of reading is understanding, and comprehension is to understanding as getting wet is to swimming. You must do the one before you can hope to do the other, but you don't do the other simply because you do the one."

—Richard Mitchell

A Note on This Chapter

If you skipped right to this section, stop for a minute. The terms and techniques discussed in this chapter will not make sense if you haven't read the book up to this point. So if you skipped the first three chapters, stop and go back to the beginning. You'll thank us later!

Conquering Comprehension

If you've ever taken a standardized test such as the SAT or GRE, you might remember what the reading comprehension questions are like. Reading comprehension shows up on practically every major standardized test, and passages are typically on obscure subjects and filled with long, winding sentences. Sometimes it seems that test writers go out of their way to find the most boring, sleep-inducing passages. They find stuff like the history of some French viscomte who researched the pupa stage of insects or the difference between a gust of wind and a gale, passages which likely have little effect on your life. Do test writers really have such strange reading habits? Probably not; but they choose these strange passages to avoid skewing the test in favor of one person or another.

For example, what if a test writer chose a passage on auto mechanics? Every test taker who didn't know a bunch about cars would be at a huge disadvantage. What about a passage on baseball? Everyone who wasn't a fan would do much worse than the other people. By choosing a strange topic, attached to no specific group, and unusual enough that few people will know it anyway, they guarantee that most people are at the same disadvantage—it mystifies everyone equally. However, if you yourself happen to know the fluctuations of the jet stream backwards and forwards, you might just hit the jackpot! Don't count on it, though. You're not supposed to be familiar with the information in a passage—so remain calm.

Anyone who is driven to jitters by a standardized test is cheating themselves out of points. The reading comprehension questions are intended to make you want to tear you hair out, so when you see a passage on the migration pattern of the Crested Wallabee or the rate of plaque buildup on a dog's teeth, you should have one reaction—"I got this." Others around you may be banging their heads against their desks, trying to get excused from the test, looking to cheat off of the smartest kid in the class. You don't have to do any of these things. You're learning how to "read smart."

Facts vs. Themes

Before you read any passage, **pre-read the questions.** There are two types of questions on reading passages—*fact* questions and *theme* questions. A fact question is "In what year did Eli Whitney invent the cotton gin?" or "Martha's husband was named _____." A fact question tells you what to look for.

Theme questions are "The main point of the passage is" or "Which, if true, most undermines the author's argument?" Fact questions can be quickly and easily searched out in the passage. Theme questions cannot. When you first go through the questions, don't worry about the specific information. Just look for whether it is a *fact* question or a *theme* question. Mark an "F" next to fact questions and a "T" next to theme questions. You're going to deal with each of these types of questions differently.

First the Facts...

Go after *every* fact question. It's rare that we tell you to do everything, but you should answer every one of them, because the answers are all right in the passage. Scan the passage looking for words that quickly tell you where the answer is. These kind of words are called **stop signs**, because they show you where you should stop and look for the answer.

For example, here's the Eli Whitney question again: "In what year did Eli Whitney invent the cotton gin?" Why not look for Whitney, cotton gin, or all the dates in the passage? **Don't even read the sentences.** Just look for key words. If they don't tell you the answer, move on to the next stop sign. Fact questions are free points on a test—they are straightforward and easily handled. Use the stop signs to answer them efficiently and rake in the points.

...Then the Themes

Once you've answered all the fact questions, go back and read the passage. Keep in mind the type of theme question you're going to need to answer. Are you going to need to know the main point of the passage? How about reasons which lead to the conclusion of the passage? You are still going to be looking for information, but, unfortunately, it won't be as easy as looking for simple facts.

Are you going to read the whole passage? Nope. Read only the first paragraph and the first sentence of each subsequent paragraph. Usually, the first sentence will clearly tell you about what is going to follow. If the paragraphs are long, read the last sentence as well. If you still don't get the main idea, then keep reading until you do. Last, read the entire final paragraph. Don't pay attention to details, names, and dates when theme reading—pay attention to ideas, arguments, and direction. Finding out the author's argument is critical to answering theme questions.

Reading Zone 4.1

Read the following passage and then answer the questions that follow. You can check your answers on page 236.

> The crucial years of the Depression, as they are brought into historical focus, increasingly emerge as the decisive decade for American art, if not for American culture in general. For it was during this decade that many of the conflicts which had blocked the progress of American art in the past came to a head and sometimes boiled over. Janus-faced, the thirties look backward, sometimes as far as the Renaissance; and at the same time forward, as far as the present and beyond. It was the moment when artists, like Thomas Hart Benton, who wished to turn back the clock to regain the virtues of simpler times came into direct conflict with others, like Stuart Davis and Frank Lloyd Wright, who were ready to come to terms with the Machine Age and to deal with its consequences.

America in the thirties was changing rapidly. In many areas, the past was giving way to the present, although not without a struggle. A predominantly rural and small town society was being replaced by the giant complexes of the big cities; power was becoming increasingly centralized in the federal government and in large corporations. As a result, traditional American types such as the independent farmer and the small business man were being replaced by the executive and the bureaucrat. Many Americans, deeply attached to the old way of life, felt disinherited. At the same time, as immigration decreased and the population became more homogeneous, the need arose in art and literature to commemorate the ethnic and regional differences that were fast disappearing. The incursions of government controls on the laissez-faire system, acting to erode the Calvinist ethic of hard work and personal sacrifice on which both the economy and public morality had rested, called forth a similar reaction. Thus, paradoxically, the conviction that art, at least, should serve some purpose or carry some message of moral uplift grew stronger as the Puritan ethos lost its contemporary reality. Often this elevating message was a sermon in favor of just those traditional American virtues which were now threatened with obsolescence in a changed social and political context.

In this new context, the appeal of the paintings by the Regionalists and the American Scene painters often lay in their ability to recreate an atmosphere that glorified the traditional American values—self-reliance tempered with good-neighborliness, independence modified by a sense of community, hard work rewarded by a sense of order and purpose. Given the actual temper of the times, these themes were strangely anachronistic, just as the rhetoric supporting political isolationism was equally inappropriate in an international situation soon to involve America in a second world war. Such themes gained popularity because they filled a genuine need for a comfortable collective fantasy of a God-fearing, white-picket-fence America, which in retrospect took on the nostalgic appeal of a lost Golden Age.

In this light, an autonomous art-for-art's sake was viewed as a foreign invader liable to subvert the native American desire for a purposeful art. Abstract art was assigned the role of the villainous alien; realism was to personify the genuine American means of expression. The argument drew favor in many camps: among the artists, because most were realists; among the politically oriented intellectuals, because abstract art was apolitical; and among museum officials, because they were surfeited with mediocre imitations of European modernism and were convinced that American art must develop its own distinct identity. To help along this road to self-definition, the museums were prepared to set up an artificial double standard, one for American art, and another for European art.

In 1934, Ralph Flint wrote in *Art News*, "We have today in our midst a greater array of what may be called second-, third-, and fourth-string artists than any other country. Our big annual are marvelous outpourings of intelligence and skill; they have all the diversity and animation of a five-ring circus."

The most commanding attraction in this circus was surely that of the American Scene painters, a category that may be broadened to accommodate both the urban realists, like Reginald Marsh, Isabel Bishop, Alexander Brook, and the brothers Isaac, Moses and Raphael Soyer, and the Regionalists, like Thomas Hart Benton, John Steuart Curry, and Grant Wood. American Scene painting was, to a degree, a continuation of the tradition of Henri and the New York realists, which had by no means died out. Its stronghold was the Art Students League, where John Sloan was elected director in 1931, and Kenneth Hays Miller and Yasui Kuniyoshi, also former Henri students, perpetuated Henri's approach. Here, too, Thomas Hart Benton preached the gospel of Regionalism.

1. According to the passage, one painter from the "urban realist" school was
   (A) Grant Wood
   (B) Thomas Hart Benton
   (C) Joan Sloan
   (D) Isaac Soyer
   (E) Isabel Bishop

2. According to the passage, in the 1930s, abstract art was seen as
   (A) uniquely American
   (B) uniquely European
   (C) relevant to post-war traumaticism
   (D) imitative of European modernism
   (E) counter to American regionalism

3. American Scene painters were characterized by
   (A) landscape painting
   (B) abstract painting
   (C) representing American values
   (D) exploring an atmosphere of internationalism
   (E) depicting religious sentiment

4. In 1931, the director of the Art Students League was
   (A) Ralph Flint
   (B) Kenneth Hayes Miller
   (C) Thomas Hart Benton
   (D) John Sloan
   (E) John Steuart Curry

5. The "artificial double standard" mention in the passage refers to

   (A) the difference between standards of judgment for European art and American art
   (B) the difference between standards of judgment for realism and abstract art
   (C) the difference between museum officials and the common American perception
   (D) the distinction between art's movement toward Puritanism and America's movement toward hedonism
   (E) the difference between standards of judgment for politically oriented intellectuals and museum officials

6. According to the passage, one artist who advocated a return to earlier values was

   (A) John Steuart Curry
   (B) Thomas Hart Benton
   (C) John Calvin
   (D) Raphael Soyer
   (E) Ralph Flint

7. The best word to describe America in the 1930s would be

   (A) reactionary
   (B) consistent
   (C) dynamic
   (D) stolid
   (E) melancholic

8. According to the passage, one response to industrialization was

   (A) abstract art
   (B) a conservative movement in art
   (C) a movement toward mobile art
   (D) an abandonment of art
   (E) a removal from European influences

9. According to the passage, Stuart Davis was a representative of
   (A) regionalism responding in art
   (B) dadaism as the future of art
   (C) modernism as included in art
   (D) futurism as expressed through art
   (E) industrialization accepted by art

10. The best choice for title of the above passage would be
    (A) "The Thirties in Art: Reaction and Rebellion"
    (B) "America in the Thirties: A Changing Time"
    (C) "Thomas Hart Benton and Regionalism"
    (D) "Art, Politics, and Growth in America"
    (E) "The Art Students League: A History"

Reflection

For any question you got wrong, go back and leave notes next to each answer choice indicating why it is correct or incorrect. It's important that you not only practice, but also reflect on your performance! This way, you'll see what issues give you trouble and gain a better understanding of how to improve.

Did pre-reading help you get through the passage faster? Without pre-reading, you would have read the passage and when you came to fact questions, you would have had to go back to the passage, likely more than once, to look up the answers. The point is, burying yourself in a passage without knowing what you are going to need it for is a useless exercise. It's like reading anything. You have to know why you are reading it. Theme questions are more difficult to pin down, but by knowing them before you read, you can look for them and let them guide you through the piece.

Pick and Choose

Most passages contain a whole bunch of useless information (in other words, information that you don't need to know in order to answer the questions at the end). Reading the questions first is a great way to get around this worthless information. Also, avoid reading the whole lists of anything, whether they are names, dates, groups, or countries. Another thing to look out for is the interesting stuff in the passage because it is usually *not* what you will be tested on. If there is a hilariously funny description of Ryan Seacrest covered in chocolate and feathers, you can be certain that the questions will ask only about what he studied in college. Be careful not to get drawn in by any interesting, but secondary, information. Don't be fooled—test writers were not put on this earth to entertain you.

Watch That Turn

Remember when we told you how facts become stop signs that tell you to read that particular section? Well, there are **turn signs** as well. Look out for words which indicate a change in opinion, or a reversal of direction. Words like **although, however, but,** and **in spite of** (anything which indicates a change of opinion) tell you that whatever the main point was in the previous section, a different point will take place in succeeding paragraphs. Circling these turn sign words will help you keep the argument's direction in mind.

Mini-Mapping

These turn sign words are crucial to our final reading technique called **mini-mapping**. You'll learn more about mapping, or making an outline of an author's argument, in Chapter 11. Mini-mapping does the same thing but is less specific and detailed.

Read the first paragraph. From the first paragraph you should be able to figure out the thesis for the entire passage. Summarize the thesis of the passage in the margin. For each subsequent paragraph, write next to it what job that paragraph does, keeping in mind it can only do a few things:

(1) It can **support the thesis**.

(2) It can **provide an example** of the thesis.

(3) It can **attack the thesis**.

(4) It can **provide a different opinion** from the thesis.

Everything else the paragraph may do is not useful for theme questions, so, if a paragraph doesn't do any of these things, ignore it. Mini-mapping quickly tells you where to go to answer theme questions. Think of it this way: The difference between mapping and mini-mapping is like the difference between a big, beautiful atlas map and a map you scanned from a placemat from a fast-food restaurant. Although they may both cover the same geographical region, one is much more specific and detailed than the other. One is more useful for planning a long trip, while the other is more useful for getting a general idea of the landscape. Mini-mapping also gives you a quick snapshot of the extent to which the passage supports or attacks an argument.

Reading Zone 4.2

Read the following passage and then answer the questions that follow. You can check your answers on page 237.

BREACH OF FAITH

In June 1972, the District of Columbia police took into custody five burglars who had broken into the offices of the Democratic National Committee at the fashionable Watergate complex in Washington, apparently to plant a listening device. A trail of clues led incredibly from the perpetrators—three Cuban émigrés and two native-born Americans, all with CIA connections—to E. Howard Hunt, an administration consultant who a dozen years earlier had helped plan the Bay of Pigs invasion, and to G. Gordon Liddy, a Republican campaign official. All seven men were indicted. The head of the Nixon campaign committee, the president's close friend, former Attorney General John Mitchell, denied prior knowledge but resigned all the same.

As the Watergate Seven awaited trial that fall, the Democrats attempted unsuccessfully to make an issue of the episode. The American electorate, apparently unwilling to face the prospect of a McGovern presidency, behaved almost as a willing conspirator in the increasingly dubious pretense that the break-in had been the work of a few overzealous underlings. In fact, Nixon himself had secretly allowed his top domestic aid, H.R. Haldeman, to dissuade the FBI from a serious investigation that would have demonstrated otherwise.

Throughout 1973 and into 1974, the cover-up slowly came apart, partly because of pressure from a determined opposition, partly because Nixon and those around him displayed monumental ineptitude and inexplicable irresolution in dealing with a matter of political life and death. The events are well known: the conviction of the original Watergate burglars; the decision of their leader to implicate hitherto untouched administration figures; an investigation conducted by a special Senate committee headed by Sam Ervin of North Carolina; indictments of more administration figures; the resignations of FBI director L. Patrick Gray and Attorney General Richard Kleindienst; the appointment of Archibald Cox as special prosecutor; the discovery that the president had taped most of his confidential conversation; the inexorable push to make the tapes public; the Saturday Night Massacre firing of Cox and others in October, 1973; the conviction of various administration officials on charges such as perjury and obstruction of justice; continued pressure from a new special prosecutor, Leon Jaworski; the issuance of some "sanitized" transcripts; court orders mandating full release of the tapes. Along the way, there also occurred the forced resignation of Vice-President Agnew under charges of taking illegal payoffs, an Internal Revenue Service assessment against the president for back taxes, and the revelation that some of the Watergate burglars had been part of a White House "plumbers" unit that had engaged in other illegal activities. During the last week of July 1974, the House Judiciary Committee recommended impeachment. A few days later, Nixon was forced by his own angry Lawyers to release the "smoking gun" transcript of June 23, 1972, proving conclusively that the president long had known about cover-up efforts. On August 8, 1974, he became the first chief executive in American history to resign from office.

As with any series of events played out on the level of epic human drama, Watergate was utterly fascinating in itself—for its human interest, its complexity, and its alteration of the course of American history. Beyond the public view of powerful men parading from the Senate committee rooms to the courtrooms and thence to public disgrace, however, there remain compelling questions. How could Watergate have happened in the first place? And how could a trivial surreptitious entry about which a president almost certainly had no advance knowledge be allowed to become a national obsession for nearly a year and a half? And how could this obsession bring down a leader who had been elected by overwhelming majorities? The answers appear to reside within Richard Nixon—in his own insecure, meanspirited personality and the responses it aroused.

1. According to the passage, the action initially responsible for the downfall of President Nixon was
   (A) the Bay of Pigs
   (B) the Watergate break-in
   (C) the taping of confidential conversations
   (D) the hiring of E. Howard Hunt
   (E) the firing of the independent prosecutor

2. The term "smoking gun," as used in the passage, implies
   (A) information which led to discovery of the break-in
   (B) information which led to resignation of the FBI director
   (C) the weapon used by Nixon to kill himself
   (D) information which proved Nixon's culpability
   (E) information which implicated Nixon's participation in the break-in

3. The name of the *second* special prosecutor was
   (A) Leon Jaworski
   (B) L. Patrick Gray
   (C) Archibald Cox
   (D) Sam Ervin
   (E) Spiro Agnew

4. The purpose of the initial break-in at the Watergate Hotel was to
   (A) spy on the Democrats
   (B) plant an agent at the Democratic National Convention
   (C) steal documentation outlining the Democrats' plans for the upcoming election
   (D) assassinate George McGovern, the Democratic candidate
   (E) plant listening devices

5. The special senate committee was headed by
   (A) Archibald Cox
   (B) Sam Ervin
   (C) G. Gordon Liddy
   (D) L. Patrick Gray
   (E) Richard Kleindienst

6. Which of the following, if true, most supports the author's position?
   (A) The FBI was later cleared of any complicity in covering up the break-in.
   (B) President Gerald Ford subsequently pardoned Richard Nixon.
   (C) Richard Nixon grew up insecure and unsure of his position in life.
   (D) Pat Nixon, Richard's wife, was a Rhodes scholar.
   (E) Archibald Cox later suggested that he was fired because he was discovering the truth.

7. Who, according to the passage, was most responsible for the downfall of President Nixon?
   (A) E. Howard Hunt
   (B) G. Gordon Liddy
   (C) John Mitchell
   (D) Spiro Agnew
   (E) Richard Nixon

8. Which member of the Nixon advisers was integral in the planning of the Bay of Pigs invasion?
   (A) Richard Kleindienst
   (B) G. Gordon Liddy
   (C) Sam Ervin
   (D) E. Howard Hunt
   (E) L. Patrick Gray

9. The title *Breach of Faith* refers to
   (A) the disregard of the president for the electorate
   (B) the disregard of the prosecutors for the president
   (C) the disregard of members of the cabinet for the president
   (D) the disregard of the Republican Party for the Democratic Party
   (E) all of the above

10. The "Saturday Night Massacre" mentioned in the passage refers to
   (A) the resignation of major cabinet officials in the face of potential prosecution
   (B) the firing of major cabinet officials in the face of potential prosecution
   (C) the firing of Archibald Cox and the special prosecutors
   (D) the firing of Leon Jaworski and the special prosecutors
   (E) the resignation of L. Patrick Gray and Richard Kleindienst in the face of potential prosecution

Reflection

For any question you got wrong, go back and leave notes next to each answer choice indicating why it is correct or incorrect. It's important that you not only practice, but also reflect on your performance! This way, you'll see what issues give you trouble and gain a better understanding of how to improve.

Keep Your Cool

A final note on reading comprehension: The reason most people do poorly on reading passages has nothing to do with their reading speed. It has to do with the way they take tests. They panic, reread things, jump around the passage, sweat, and concentrate on the feeling that they are getting beat up on a test. We have some good advice for people who panic on tests, especially on tests with reading passages: DON'T DO IT!

Things to Take with You

1. It's not one thought that makes you panic on a test—it's an uncontrolled rush of many thoughts. If you find yourself starting to think about panicking, find some easy, common thing to take your mind off the problem. It's worth the ten seconds it takes to count the number of fingers on your hand, take a deep breath, and come back to the passage.

2. If you find a couple of questions you can't answer in a row, don't panic. That happens to everyone. Move on to other questions and come back to them later. The passage isn't going to change. Be careful and accurate.

3. If the passage is so dull you can't bear to look at it, take heart. It's like that for everyone. By pre-reading and mini-mapping, you have a huge advantage over everyone else in the room. That should make you happy, not panicked.

Reading Zone 4.3

Read the following passage and then answer the questions that follow. You can check your answers on page 238.

October 31

A week ago I laughed myself silly over Macy's "Elf Wanted" ad; this afternoon I sat in the SantaLand office and was told, "Congratulations, Mr. Sedaris, you're an elf."

In order to become an elf, I had to fill out ten pages of forms, take a multiple-choice personality test, undergo two interviews, and submit urine for a drug test. The first interview was general, designed to eliminate the obvious sociopaths. During the second interview we were asked why we wanted to be elves, which, when you think about it, is a fairly tough question. When the woman next to me, a former waitress in her late twenties, answered, she put question marks after everything she said. "I really want to be an elf? Because I think it's really about acting? And before this I worked in a restaurant? Which was owned by this really wonderful woman who had a dream to open a restaurant? And it made me think that it's like, really, really important? To have a dream?"

I told the interviewers that I wanted to be an elf because it was the most ridiculous thing I had ever heard of. I figured that for once in my life I would be completely honest and see how far it got me. I also failed the drug test. But they hired me anyway. Honesty had nothing to do with it. They hired me because I am five feet five inches tall.

November 19

Today we began our elf training. We learned the name of the various elf positions. You can be, for example, an "Oh, my God!" elf and stand at the corner near the escalator. People arrive, see the long line around the corner, and say, "Oh, my God!"; your job is to tell them that it won't take more than an hour to see Santa.

You can be an Entrance Elf, a Watercooler Elf, a Bridge Elf, Train Elf, Maze Elf, Island Elf, Magic-Window Elf, Emergency-Exit Elf, Counter Elf, Magic-Tree

Elf, Pointer Elf, Santa Elf, Photo Elf, Usher Elf, Cash-Register Elf, or Exit Elf. We were given a demonstration of the various positions, acted out by returning elves who were so "on stage" and goofy that it made me a little sick to my stomach. I didn't know that I could look anyone in the eye and exclaim, "Oh, my goodness, I think I see Santa!" or, "Can you close your eyes and make a very special Christmas wish!" It makes one's mouth hurt to speak with such forced merriment. It embarrasses me to hear people talk this way. I prefer being frank with children. I'm more likely to say, "You must be exhausted" or, "I know a lot of people who would kill for that little waistline of yours."

I am afraid I won't be able to provide the enthusiasm Santa is asking for. I think I'll be a low-key sort of elf.

November 21
My costume is green. I wear green velvet knickers, a yellow turtleneck, a forest-green velvet smock, and a perky little hat decorated with spangles. This is my work uniform.

Today was elf dress rehearsal. I worked as a Santa Elf for house number two. A Santa Elf greets children at the Magic Tree and leads them to Santa's house. When you work as a Santa Elf you have to go by your elf name. My elf name is Crumpet. The other Santa Elves have names like Jingle and Frosty. They take the children by the hand and squeal with forced delight. They sing and prance and behave like cartoon characters come to life. They frighten me.

1. The tone of the author is best described as
   (A) jocular
   (B) ironic
   (C) desperate
   (D) angry
   (E) pedantic

2. The author's "elf name" is
   (A) Creamy
   (B) Dreamboat
   (C) Strumpet
   (D) Trumpet
   (E) Crumpet

3. According to the passage, what was the author's reason for wanting to be an elf?
   (A) He needed the health benefits.
   (B) He wanted to open a restaurant.
   (C) He still believed in Santa.
   (D) He needed the money.
   (E) He thought it the most ridiculous job in the world.

4. According to the passage, why was he chosen to be an elf by management?
   (A) He was honest.
   (B) He loved Christmas.
   (C) He passed the drug test.
   (D) He was the right physical type.
   (E) He had the shoes already.

5. All of the following are elf positions at Macy's EXCEPT
   (A) Escalator Elf
   (B) Emergency-Exit Elf
   (C) Watercooler Elf
   (D) Cash Register Elf
   (E) Train Elf

6. The job the author received was
   (A) Magic-Window Elf
   (B) Santa Elf
   (C) Maze Elf
   (D) Island Elf
   (E) Pointer Elf

7. The author's knickers were
   (A) forest green
   (B) velvet yellow
   (C) velvet green
   (D) red and green
   (E) spangled green

8. The author can best be described as
   (A) a spunky elf
   (B) a low-key elf
   (C) an enthusiastic elf
   (D) an unenthusiastic elf
   (E) a frightened elf

9. Why did the woman next to the author at his second interview want to be an elf?
   (A) She loved children.
   (B) She loved Christmas.
   (C) She was a flake.
   (D) She was fired from her restaurant.
   (E) She never really answered the question.

10. This piece would most likely be found in
    (A) a diary
    (B) a newspaper article
    (C) a textbook
    (D) a gossip column
    (E) a novel

Reflection

For any question you got wrong, go back and leave notes next to each answer choice indicating why it is correct or incorrect. It's important that you not only practice, but also reflect on your performance! This way, you'll see what issues give you trouble and gain a better understanding of how to improve.

Chapter 4 Summary

- Reading comprehension passages on standardized tests like the SAT or GRE are often on obscure topics, which is probably a deliberate choice by the test writers. However, it's possible to do well on reading comprehension questions, even when the material is foreign to you.

- Before you even read the passage, read the questions. We call this pre-reading.

- Determine which questions are "fact" questions and which are "theme" questions. Fact questions are generally straightforward; the answers can be found in the passage. Theme questions, however, require you to make inferences and have a deeper understanding of the passage as a whole.

- While reading, look for key words and phrases. Don't get drawn in by all the peripheral information that's there to distract you.

- Use the mini-mapping strategy to outline the author's argument and determine the key points.

- Don't allow yourself to be intimidated by the passages. Panic and stress will just mess you up, so remain calm. If you can't answer a question right away, move on and come back to it later.

CHAPTER 5

Tweets and Telegrams

> "... It was the idea of facing a future skimming the surface of life, winging my way in and out of other people's crises, confusions, and passages, engaging them enough to get the story, but never enough to be indelibly touched by what I had seen or heard."
>
> —Anna Quindlen

The Skinny on Skimming

So far, much of this book has been interested in helping you do something analogous to actually working in order to make money. Nice and honest. This chapter is designed to help you do something analogous to breaking into a bank and stealing money quickly. To borrow Anna Quindlen's description (which, in case you missed it, is on the previous page), sometimes you want to be indelibly touched by what you have seen and heard, but other times, "it's enough to get the story."

When you don't have much time and you have to read a text, you should employ an important strategy called **skimming**. We're sure you've heard about skimming in various forms, and in practice, you probably already skim unconsciously. While skimming is always a second-best alternative to reading carefully and efficiently, believe us, we understand that people don't always have enough time to do things the right way. In our everyday lives, very often we're forced into various forms of skimming and taking shortcuts to get things done more quickly. When it comes to reading, however, you should skim only when you really need to.

Skimming Textbooks

First, recognize that of all types of skimming, this type—textbook skimming—is going to be the hardest to pull off. You don't have a plot to grab on to, the book is usually condensed stuff, so almost everything is important, and if it's a science text, you've got concepts and equations to deal with as well. Should you give up hope, quit reading altogether and just bemoan your life on social media? Of course not. We'll break up textbook skimming into main categories: social science texts and hard science texts.

Social Science Texts

Read the chapter headings and the bolded section headings. Use those to make a quick outline of each chapter. If a second heading is not clear to you, translate it into something meaningful. For example, if you have a section heading in a book on the French Revolution that says "Mme. Guillotine Collects Her Bill," you want to read that section and translate it into something, perhaps, that reads "After the revolution, the Jacobins started beheading everyone." Not as pretty, but much more useful on a test. The point is to only read if you don't understand what that section refers to. If you have to read a section, try reading the first sentence of each paragraph. If you haven't reached the main point of that paragraph, keep reading until you do. Read no further—you don't have time to read everything.

Outlining a textbook should take you a couple of hours—but then you start to see how everything relates to everything else. Pick one or two concrete examples to memorize, and hope that your teacher asks about them. Try to pick concepts that you remember the teacher discussing in class (no matter what your teachers claim, they all like to see their own words repeated back to them). Remember that seeing the overriding idea of a course or a book is more important than memorizing every date and name. A teacher teaches to an overarching concept, not a specific idea. Even if she is teaching about just the French Revolution, many books have an idea about the French Revolution that they try to support. (It wasn't a revolution; it was brought about by radicals; it was funded by the Americans; it was supported by the clergy; and so on.) Use that idea to seek out a few points on what could be an interesting essay.

Natural Science Texts

Many people gamble—they choose one topic, learn it well, cross their fingers, and walk through the doors of the classroom or testing room knowing that they will be at best only partially skewered by the exam. Skimming, on the other hand, can often save you from a lot of stress and heartache, as well as save your score.

Scientific texts usually have a summary section in the back that lists the important formulas. If it doesn't, go through each chapter looking for formulas. Find the section heading that relates to that formula. Write them down on an equation sheet. A typical entry from a chemistry textbook might look like "Heat, Temp, Size Relationship — $PV = nRT$ — P = pressure, V = volume, n = constant, R = moles of gas, T = temperature." If your test is going to be mainly quantitative, then work from this sheet. If your test is going to be conceptual, focus more on the chapter introductions and summaries. Those are the best ways to get a feel for what concepts are being examined in a chapter, and how. Read the summaries, the introductions, and the equations. Although some of the boxes with interesting information on subjects and pictures and graphs may appear fascinating, don't get sucked in. They are tangential to the main point; otherwise they would be referred to in the text. If they are referred to in the text, make sure that you can recognize and reproduce a few of them.

Skimming Journalistic Texts

Luckily, the way to skim-read journalistic reading is just how you learned to read journalism in the first place. Pre-read, read only what you need, and map the argument if it gets confusing. Know the important people, countries or industries, what the issue is, and some differing points of view on the subject.

If you must skim journalistic reading, try to picture a larger context before you begin. Let's say you have to read a nonfiction collection of articles written during the Watergate conspiracy, and it's the night before your exam. It would be helpful to remember that the Washington Post broke the scandal—so you want to pay attention to any articles from them. You want to quickly identify who was protecting Nixon and who was attacking Nixon. What examples did each type of author use to support his position? One way to picture the larger context is to divide the reading into groups, or categories. Use any category division that makes it easy to read and remember quickly. Choose one detail or one image which, for you, identifies the main point of the passage. Then, come exam day, you'll be able to say something intelligent.

Skimming Fiction

It's a last resort to skim fiction. Because fiction doesn't adhere to the "just-the-facts" method that journalism does, it's much harder to skim. That said, we have some suggestions for you.

1. Don't worry about the overall plot right away. Instead, read the first and the last chapters in their entirety. Don't worry too much about what has gone on in between. (This is like working a puzzle and starting by getting the outline pieces in order before you worry about what goes in the middle.) For now, you care about how the story begins and how it ends. What is the tone at the beginning? What is the tone at the end? Can you see any kind of progression or movement from the one to the other? Does the first chapter start off as hopeful and the last one end in unhappiness? If so, then you do in fact know something about the main shape of the narrative. Try to look for such large-scale movements.

2. Go on a plot hunt. Skim the book looking only for what happens. (If your book is of a post-modern variety, where plot is minimal or insignificant, then you can skip this step. This holds as well for works by Lawrence Sterne and absurdists.) At this point, nothing else should interest you. Jump to the beginning of each chapter and see where the characters are and what they are doing. Skip long dialogues and descriptive passages. Skip anything that doesn't further the plot. Try to see the plot as developing the progression you saw from the first chapter to the last chapter.

3. Look for images that populate the first chapter and skim the text a second time to look for those images only. Read carefully around where they appear. See if you can determine their meaning. Usually, you can make some guesses about why specific images are employed. If a bird is circling overhead at the beginning of the book, and then every time something bad happens, that same bird comes back, you can start to make some guesses as to what that bird represents. (By the way, if it's American or translated German literature, we bet it's a crow. Crows are bad news in Edgar Allen Poe poems, Franz Schubert songs, and *Game of Thrones* episodes. If you're reading translations from languages belonging to cultures that have experienced multiple drone attacks from the USA, that bird might well be an eagle.) Be careful to avoid images that are common and meaningless. Just because the sun comes up every morning and sets every evening, that doesn't mean that the author necessarily wants to impress on us the endless repetition of life when s/he mentions something about the sun. Don't *insist* on seeing meaning in everything; rather, be *open to* considering the meaning of words and phrases that come back and seem out of the ordinary.

A note here on those "skim-books" you might see at bookstores, or more likely Wikipedia articles on the plots of works of fiction: Although they theoretically outline and explain a book by summarizing the plot clearly (assuming they do that, which they don't always do), they are not very useful as a substitute for reading the text. Those books contain only the most elemental, and not necessarily accurate, ideas about a text. What if you say something on a final exam that your teacher disagrees with? Are you going to say, "But the Internet said that bluebirds were symbolic of peace?" Your teacher will set your exam book on fire, just with his or her gaze. If you must use these summaries (have you guessed by now that we don't recommend relying on them?), use them only for plot. After that, skim for images and themes *on your own.*

Tweets

While the word "tweet" originally referred to the sounds many birds make, today it more often refers to the 140-characters-or-less communication that one might send out on Twitter. ("Twitter" was originally a term used to describe certain bird songs or conversations. You know how birds don't gather their kind to tell them hour-long stories, but rather vocalize for just a few seconds? This is why terms like *Twitter* and *tweeting* can describe human communications of similarly short length.)

In the 20th century, before the Internet and even before telephones, how did people communicate most efficiently? Through telegrams. Telegrams cost money by the word. Thus, most telegrams drop everything but the nouns and verbs needed to get the message across. Which of the following telegrams would you rather pay for?

This one:

I am so dreadfully sorry, but I seem to have misplaced my wallet (at that lovely French restaurant, Chez Bouley, where I met Inez that night after the lovely absurdist play). If you could be a dear and send me some much-needed money, I would be your loving servant. I promise to remunerate you (a fancy word meaning "pay you back" when next we meet again. I hope your golf game is going well. Ta Ta—Nigel

Or this one:

Plz send $. Will repay. Nigel.

You see how much flavor is lost, but the same information gets across. It takes you much less time to read the second than the first.

The best skim-readers translate passages into telegram-like (tweet-like) information when they are really pressed for time. The secondary information and words just drop out of sight. Things like articles, prepositions, and "filler words" tend to disappear. They may be needed for flavor, but not for basic nourishment.

Exercise 5

Read the following paragraphs, translating them into telegrams/tweets in the lines below. Try to read them as telegrams/tweets, skipping the unnecessary words. You can check your answers on page 239.

1. Charles, that violent kung-fu expert, who appeared on the news last week, kicked his wall, the one with the dull brown paint, so hard, that the entire support beam shook like a scared child. He was about to kick the wall again when the roof, that rickety, thatched, poorly constructed makeshift one, fell inward, filling the air with dust and smoke. By the time those hunky, strong ambulance workers arrived on the scene, it was too late. Charles, who had lived by violence, was dead.

_____

_____

2. Stan Lee, the creator of Marvel Comics, unleashed a powerful concept even he did not imagine when he created the lovable, angry, comedic and powerful character of Iron Man. Although he intended a man of steel and technology, empowered by sophisticated weaponry and computer strategy, he did not anticipate (even in his wildest dreams) that the heart ailment he gave the main character would make the indefatigable Iron Man a hero to all those physically challenged individuals to whom crossing the street is an act of unspeakable bravery.

———————————————————————

———————————————————————

3. Clawing at the striped tie that surrounded his collared shirt, Ethan presented to his friends the image of a man gone mad. Fires burned in his eyes like the infernos of Hades, and his fingers were twisted and contorted with claw-like grips on his silk cravat. He pawed the carpet like an animal, and dashed, not knocking over any of the furniture, not bumping into any guests, but sidestepping them, panther-like, from the ballroom.

———————————————————————

———————————————————————

4. No one knew how Uncle Walvis had won the election. His campaign slogan, "Uuurk Ooogh Maaghen Nooob," was not understood by a single person, not even his campaign manager. People were certain that the photos of his wife and Michael Jackson frolicking in the surf would hurt his chances, but they didn't. Even the curses he spouted at the debate were taken as signs of his "colorful nature." Despite all the problems and the pitfalls, Uncle Walvis was on his way to Washington, after, of course, he had few drinks at the Waloon Saloon on Tenth Street.

———————————————————————

———————————————————————

By the final passage, did you start to read these in a tweet/telegram style? We hope that sometimes, or someday, you read entire passages as well and enjoy doing so; when you skim, you lose the feel of the language, a number of precise adjectives or adverbs, and some evocative imagery. But if you *must* read quickly, why not read the important stuff only? Turning prose into a telegram/tweet/text message eliminates the "unnecessary" information and increases your speed and retention.

How to Set Reading Goals

Have you ever said to yourself, say at about 1:00 P.M., "I'm just going to read until three o'clock, then I can go out and do some fun stuff." At 2:00 P.M., you take a break, get some food, check e-mail. At 2:30, you sit in your chair, with your book in your hand, daydreaming, thinking about what you're going to do at 3:00. Then, at 2:45, you start making phone calls, and admit that really, you're done reading. What can you get done in fifteen minutes?

Don't be embarrassed. That's the kind of stuff people do all the time. And it doesn't make them bad readers. But it stops them from being the best readers they could be. Instead of setting time-limit goals, set reading goals. Sounds like a little thing, huh? But people tend to finish books much faster when they set page-number goals rather than time goals.

If you have a page-number goal, it doesn't matter if you daydream, take a break, or talk on the telephone. You still will not be any closer to going out and doing something fun. You can't fake reading (unless you skim *when you don't have to*—and that's a huge waste of energy). By setting realistic reading goals every day, you guarantee that you can't even undermine yourself subconsciously. You simply have to do it. And once you start doing it, you work it into your daily schedule and it ceases to feel like so much of a chore. Get away from time goals—you'll find a way to undermine yourself by filling the time with everything *but* reading.

Widen Your Vocabulary

Something that keeps people from reading as fast as they otherwise could is a limited vocabulary. The best readers have a large vocabulary—primarily because they read and learn these new words, either in context or through explanations. The more you read, then, the more your vocabulary will expand. If you want to jump a level in terms of speed and understanding, you have to work on your vocabulary outside of reading. We haven't asked you to do any pushups or situps in this book; we haven't asked you to do outside research in linguistics or to learn a foreign language. Working on your vocabulary is a lifelong task. No one knows *every* word. But the more you know, the less likely you are to stare at a passage and say "what the heck is she talking about?"

Buy a cheap notebook. In it, keep a list of new words you learn. Again, writing things down produces the highest retention levels. Working on your vocabulary is one of those things that might be a pain for the first couple of weeks, but rapidly becomes much easier. Just keep in mind that the smartest person in the United States probably only knows two to three thousand more words than you do. That's what separates the smartest person from the average person in terms of vocabulary. By learning five hundred new words, you jump to the top twenty percent of the country. This is the kind of learning that rewards hard work.

Reading Zone 5

Skim-read the following passage and answer the questions that follow. Try to summarize and turn the passage into a tweet/telegram as you read it. You can check your answers on page 240.

Las Vegas is a good restaurant town. It's not New York or San Francisco, but it offers respectable culinary and ethnic diversity, served dependably. Las Vegas hotel dining is relatively homogeneous in style and cuisine, while proprietary restaurants try hard to be different. The restaurant business in Las Vegas is as much a psychological as a culinary art, an exercise in perceived versus real value. In Las Vegas you can have the same meal in an astounding variety of environments for an unbelievable range of prices.

Left to its own devices, Las Vegas would be a meat and potatoes town. Owing to the expectations of its many visitors, however, Las Vegas restaurants put on the dog. There are dozens of designer restaurants, gourmet rooms as they are known locally, where the pampered and the curious can pretend they are dining in an exclusive French or Continental restaurant while enjoying the food they like most: meat and potatoes. It is a town full of Ponderosas masquerading as Lutèce or The Four Seasons.

What has saved the day for discriminating diners is the increased presence of foreign visitors, particularly Asians. The needs of these visitors in conjunction with their economic clout have precipitated great growth and improvement among proprietary ethnic restaurants, which in turn have forced improvement among the more staid hotel/casino dining rooms. While many of the hotel gourmet rooms continue to be gastronomic and stylistic carbon copies, Las Vegas's proprietary restaurants have established distinct identities based on their creativity in the kitchen. There are two kinds of restaurants in Las Vegas: restaurants which are an integral part of a hotel/casino operation, and restaurants which must make it entirely on the merits of their food. Gourmet rooms in the hotels are usually associated with the casinos. Their mission is to pamper customers who are giving the house a lot of gambling action. At any given time, most of the folks in a hotel gourmet room are dining as guests of the casino. If you are a paying customer in the same restaurant, the astronomical prices you are charged help subsidize the feeding of all these comped guests. Every time you buy a meal in a gourmet room, you are helping to pay the tab of the strangers sitting at the next table. This is not to say the gourmet rooms do not serve excellent food. On the contrary, some of the best chefs in the country cook for hotel/casino gourmet rooms. The bottom line, however, if you are a paying guest, is that you are taking up space intended for high rollers, and the house is going to charge you a lot of rent.

Restaurants independent of casinos work at a considerable disadvantage. First, they do not have a captive audience of gamblers or convention-goers. Second, their operation is not subsidized by gaming, and third, they are not located where you will just stumble upon them. Finally, they not only compete with the casino gourmet rooms, but also go head-to-head with the numerous buffets and bulk-loading meal deals which casinos offer as loss-leaders to attract the less affluent gambler.

Successful proprietary restaurants in Las Vegas must offer something very distinct, very different, and very good at a competitive price, and must somehow communicate to you that they are offering it. Furthermore, their offer must be compelling enough to induce you to travel to their location, forsaking the convenience of dining in your hotel. Not easy.

All of this works to the consumer's advantage, of course. High rollers get comped in the gourmet rooms. Folks of more modest means can select from among the amazing steak, lobster, and prime rib deals offered by the casinos, or enjoy exceptional food at bargain prices at independent restaurants. People with hardly any money at all can gorge themselves on loss-leader buffets. In many ways, Las Vegas restaurants are the culinary version of free-market economy. The casinos siphon off the customers who are willing to pay big bucks for food and feed them for free. This alters the target market for the independents and serves to keep a lid on their prices. Independents providing exceptional quality for such reasonable charges ensure in turn that buffets and meal deals stay cheap. Ah, America, what a country!

1. According to the passage, proprietary restaurants in Las Vegas are
   (A) all extremely similar
   (B) run by the casinos
   (C) inordinately expensive
   (D) crowded and scattered
   (E) creative and individual

2. The phrase "put on the dog," as used in the passage, means
   (A) serve meat and potatoes
   (B) become more fancy
   (C) keep things simple
   (D) cater to tourist needs
   (E) lower prices

3. According to the author, casino restaurants have an advantage over independent restaurants because
   (A) they offer room deals that include food at a considerable discount
   (B) their operations are subsidized by gambling revenues
   (C) they attract a more wealthy client
   (D) without rent, they are able to charge lower prices
   (E) all of the above

4. According to the author, food in Las Vegas can be generally described as
   (A) expensive and unpleasant
   (B) traditional American cuisine
   (C) scattered across the Strip and difficult to get to
   (D) competitive and differentiated
   (E) usually very inexpensive

5. According to the passage, the gourmet rooms
   (A) serve food to high rollers only
   (B) are priced high, but reasonably for the food
   (C) serve French and Continental cuisine only
   (D) are staffed by some of the best chefs in the country
   (E) pay no rent, and are therefore anti-competitive

6. An adjective used in the passage to describe the overall diversity and quality of the dining experience in Las Vegas is
   (A) pricy
   (B) compelling
   (C) gourmet
   (D) free-market
   (E) respectable

7. The Las Vegas term "gourmet room" means
   (A) an expensive restaurant
   (B) a supper club for local high rollers
   (C) a buffet room, subsidized by the casino
   (D) a restaurant which serves French or Continental cuisine
   (E) a designer restaurant

8. According to the author, dining in Las Vegas would be less palatable without
   (A)   competitive pricing
   (B)   the increase in foreign visitors
   (C)   locally grown food supplies
   (D)   a variety of price-range options
   (E)   the overseeing arm of the price-control commission

9. What does the author mean by a "proprietary restaurant"?
   (A)   Privately owned
   (B)   Buffet style
   (C)   Expensive
   (D)   Exotic
   (E)   Affiliated with a casino

10. Which of the following, if true, would most undermine the author's experience of dining in Las Vegas?
    (A)   He contracted botulism from a bowl of soup at the Sands casino.
    (B)   He couldn't get a reservation at Wolfgang Puck's cafe.
    (C)   There is no ethnic cuisine in Las Vegas.
    (D)   Las Vegas charges a minimum food tax of 73%.
    (E)   The average restaurant in Las Vegas closes after three months of operation.

Reflection

For any question you got wrong, go back and leave notes next to each answer choice indicating why it is correct or incorrect. It's important that you not only practice, but also reflect on your performance! This way, you'll see what issues give you trouble and gain a better understanding of how to improve.

Chapter 5 Summary

- Though not nearly as efficient as reading carefully and thoroughly, skimming a text is an option when you're pressed for time.

- Your skimming strategy will shift depending on the text—is it academic, journalistic, or narrative?

- Tweeting can be thought of as more than just digital shorthand. Effective tweeting requires skills in summarization and the ability to condense a lot of information, eliminating the "filler" words.

- Expanding your vocabulary will help you read more effectively and quickly, as you won't need to go searching for definitions or spend a lot of time trying to figure out the meaning of a word or sentence.

PART II

Reading Specific Text Types

Natural Sciences

"I do not know whether you are fond of chemical reading.
There are some things in this science worth reading."

—Thomas Jefferson

Tackling Scientific Texts

Some of the most dense, challenging writing you may ever come across is that in scientific texts, whether a textbook, manual, or journal article. Science texts are usually packed with tough concepts, unfamiliar terminology, and occasionally, long, winding sentences. This chapter contains a few straightforward strategies for reading and comprehending these information-dense texts.

Use Your Pen/Pencil

A good way to make sure you are not just blindly reading facts is to read every textbook with your pen in hand. In the margin, jot down the main idea of the section, and when you get to the part of that paragraph that relates to the main idea, underline it. Then circle the facts you'll need to memorize later. Distinguish quickly between reading and studying. Reading should give you the overall picture presented by the facts; studying is the way to memorize the facts themselves.

For any discipline, the facts are useful, but they are not the most important part of any course of study. An overwhelming number of people try to memorize facts as they read them. Every fact. Every date. Every name. That is what we have textbooks for—to keep track of all that stuff. Work to distinguish reading from sheer memorization, comprehension from studying. On a first read of any textbook, your primary goal should be understanding the relationship between parts, the main point, and the direction of the text.

Pre-Read for Profit

The most effective way of checking out where the book is heading before you read it is to pre-read the chapter. **Pre-reading** is looking ahead at all the clues the text provides to describe what kind of material you are about to read. First, look at the title of the chapter. Does it spell out the larger concept that will be covered in the chapter? A physics textbook offers some of the following chapter headings: "Newton's Second Law: Gravitation," "Work and Energy," and "Heat Transfer." When you study these chapters, you should understand that the information contained within will pertain to these topics and, in your mind, associate them easily with the equations or subheadings. Say to yourself, "Oh, gravitation. The idea of orbiting bodies, and why things fall are both just parts of gravitation. One is between planets, the other is on planets."

In each chapter, there may be subheadings for sections or paragraphs. You should quickly read all the subheadings, centered or bolded as they may be, to get a quick idea of how the ideas are going to progress. You've seen examples here in this book. Go back through the first few chapters, looking at the subheadings. They should give you a pretty good idea of what comes right after each one. Try pre-reading for the rest of this book. You'll be glad you did. If your textbook contains questions at the end of each chapter, read them before you begin the chapter. It's like your teacher telling you what's going to be on the final exam before the class begins. Take the hint—make sure you look for that stuff aggressively before you read the chapter. One of the most difficult things to do in textbooks is to figure out on your first read what is important and what you can whiz by. These questions are your road map through the passage.

The Scientific Method

In scientific texts, don't worry about the questions that merely serve to reinforce your ability to manipulate a set of equations when pre-reading. Look for questions that ask about larger themes and overarching principles, not just plug-ins or word problems. Those are useful, but not as pre-reading. Pre-reading is designed to help you anticipate a line of thought—not to resolve its every intricacy.

By now, you're beginning to see a split in how you should approach scientific texts and social-scientific texts, like math versus history. Each type has some problems and idiosyncrasies unique to it, and a closer look at each will clear some of them up.

Straightforward Science

In scientific texts, the authors will begin with the fundamentals of the discipline and the build from there. The first few chapters should provide you with most of the background that you will need for all later chapters, so if you are going to spend more time on any one part, make it the beginning. Unfortunately, the beginning chapters are usually dull because, well, background information is usually dull. Still, it's important that you don't skip ahead to the exciting stuff without knowing the basics. (You also don't want to be in a situation where the background information you skipped shows up on a test or work project, for instance.) Jumping into a difficult textbook midstream is like deciding you're going to become a doctor by practicing surgery on yourself. There are certain things you really need to know, and you're going to get hurt if you don't.

Make a Mess

Some people act as though texts should remain pristine and untouched. Certainly your library does. If you are going to use a text often, get your own copy, because useful reading in scientific texts is done not only with the eyes, but also with a pen. Mark up the book, underline, take notes. We cannot emphasize enough that this will improve your reading. When you annotate as you read, you will not only know what is important to study when finals come around, for example, but also where the good examples are that explain abstract principles. Gravity, for instance, is such a nebulous concept that when explained in abstract terms, it is easily misconstrued. But if you can think of gravity as a giant vacuum, sucking everything toward its center, then all of a sudden you have a concrete image of the effects of gravity, and it becomes easier to remember.

Mark up your books and take notes in them. Even if you doodle, do it around important ideas or concepts. Then you have something to identify the concept with. Unmarked books are useless during review time. Each page looks like every other page, with nothing to identify it for you. By circling facts, by noting important ideas in the margin, you increase the chance that they will stay in your head; you'll be able to picture the things you circled on the page or wrote in the margin.

In scientific texts, ideas are usually broken into one idea per paragraph. Identifying that idea and summarizing it in the margin next to the paragraph is a good idea. In that way, you construct an outline of the chapter while reading it. When you need to memorize the important information from the chapter, you have an outline at your fingertips. If this sounds overwhelming, just think of all the work and stress it may save you later on.

Words In Context

Most dense texts have their own language, their own specific vocabulary. Do you need to know the precise meaning of every term? Hardly. Of course, it doesn't hurt to look up words you don't know, especially words that appear over and over again in a text. Technical jargon has the effect of droning you to sleep, making you feel lost and confused, and deflating your aggressive attitude in approaching the material. Do not let this stop you from being a more effective reader.

The key to getting around technical jargon is twofold. First, stopping at every word and looking it up is counterproductive. By letting the word reveal itself in context, you can keep your reading rhythm without stopping and starting. This first technique is important for keeping the fluidity (and therefore the pace) of your reading as continuous as possible.

Read the following passage and see if you can figure out the meaning of the word without knowing exactly what is being described.

> *Criatus Micanscropus* uses all eight legs to support its weight. Though too small to be seen by the human eye, its sting can raise small welts and can be thought of as a mosquito by the uninitiated. *Criatus Micanscropus* lives in colonies of 7–12, and it thrives on scalp decay, skin detritus, and spins minute webs which, if embedded in the dermic layer, can cause infection.

Can you picture a tiny, spiderlike bug? It is tough to train yourself to keep reading when you don't recognize a word, but it is important that you don't get bogged (or bugged, in this case) down by unfamiliar terms. By letting words reveal themselves in context, you avoid getting thrown by what you don't immediately recognize. The following exercise tests your ability to determine the meaning of words based on a given context.

Exercise 6.1

Try to figure out what's being described in bold, and put your answer in the blank underneath the question. We've done the first one for you. Remember, you can check your answers on page 241.

1. **To engage the selective-access unit, insert one of the provided selective-access unit actuators into the selective-access unit actuator slot and rotate until the access-denial bolt has audibly engaged. To disengage the access-denial bolt, reverse procedure.**

   a lock and key

2. The adventurous traveler crossed **any half of the Earth's surface.**

   _____

3. Polar bears and penguins are apt to be found in the **region in the northernmost area of the Earth.**

   _____

4. Charles looked for his eventual destination, the heart of Africa, in his **bound collection of maps.**

   _____

5. While strolling through the department store, Jennifer casually picked up a fifteen-dollar bracelet and slipped it into her purse without paying. Jennifer suffered from **a compulsion to steal, usually without economic need.**

   _____

6. The days of the specialized craftsman for popularly accessible goods is gone; once Henry Ford made his presence known, nothing has worked more effectively than **a linear grouping of factory workers and equipment along which a product being assembled passes consecutively from operation to operation until complete.**

_____

7. The difficulty with the physics of the waterslide rests on one basic principle: **the resistance of an object to the medium through which or on which it is traveling.**

_____

8. As an editor, Laurice worked daily with **an often sextagonal, long stem of graphite surrounded by wood, occasionally tipped on one end by vulcanized rubber.**

_____

9. Any operation on the trachea must take into account the proximity of the **two folds of tissue located in the larynx that vibrate when air passes over them.** If those folds of tissue are damaged, speech patterns could become impaired.

_____

10. Aside from his mutton-chopped later incarnation, initially this **American rock-and-roll singer of the twentieth century known for his distinctive throaty tone in which songs as "Hound Dog"** was viewed as both the primary American clean-cut rebellious sex symbol and as a patriotic member of our armed forces.

_____

People don't always write as simply as or as clearly as they should. It's up to you to make sense of their long-winded gibberish. By figuring out words in context, you save yourself a trip to the dictionary and keep your focus on what you're reading. Whenever you stop reading and do something else, you become disengaged from the book, article, or whatever it is that you're reading. For example, if, while eating, you tasted a spice you couldn't identify, would you get up in the middle of the meal and go through the spice rack to figure out what spice it was? No, because your food would get cold. Similarly, your concentration and engagement with a piece of writing becomes "cold" when you step away from it for a period of time. Therefore, when you're reading, use the context to tell you the word, and later you can look up a textbook definition. Keep your focus on the text.

Translation

In addition to pre-reading, an important technique for comprehension is called **translation**. Translation involves taking a piece of technical jargon and identifying it with a commonsense phrase or definition in your mind. Then, every time you see this phrase, you link it with a definition that makes sense. Most technical books are written by people who have an expertise in a particular discipline. These people have no sympathy for our lack of knowledge. They are so far removed from common vocabulary problems that they don't even realize there could possibly be a problem. It's up to you to turn their technical stuff into meaningful words.

Let's look at an example. Read the following passage and look at how we would translate it.

A property of matter that is closely related to mass is mass density. Mass density refers to the amount of matter in a given amount of space and is defined as the mass per unit volume of a substance.

Clear? No, not to us either. It might be more helpful if it were translated into the following:

> Density is matter per amount of space. Hmm. Well, density is just the amount of stuff in a space. If I have a lot of stuff, something is very dense. If I have a little bit of stuff in the same space, it's not very dense. It's like my room. If I have a bunch of my clothes and stuff all over, it is tough to navigate through my room. If there is just a little bit of stuff, it is easy to get through my room. Density, then, is just clutter.

Now, for some of you, this definition will be equally useless. The key is to find the definition that makes sense for you. Then, every time you see "density," you can say, "Oh, that's just clutter," and all that the definition means for you.

You wouldn't write this entire paragraph in the margin. What you would do is figure this out in your hand, and then write in the margin "Density = Clutter." The next time you see the word "density," you'll think "clutter."

The more you translate, the less mystical complex subjects will appear to you. What does this have to do with reading? A lot. Reading is making sense of symbols. The harder your brain has to work to translate symbols, the slower you will read. Translation is a way of speeding up that process.

Exercise 6.2

Read the passages that follow. Then, on the lines below each passage, summarize the passage, translating the technical jargon and terminology into everyday language. You can check your answers on page 241.

1. Heating a mixture of substances usually provides activation energy and increases the rate of chemical reaction. A high temperature would not be a good way for a cell to obtain activation energy. Too much heat would harm a cell. It might produce reactions that would cause cells to disintegrate. There is one way to increase the rate of reactions, however, that is not harmful. When certain chemicals, called catalysts (CAT-uhlists), are present, molecules can interact without the need for extra heat. This means that catalysts act to lower the amount of activation energy needed.

_____

_____

_____

_____

2. The Nichiren Sect

This is a Japanese sect, founded in the thirteenth century by Nichiren, a fiery patriot who thought he had discovered original Buddhism in the Lotus of the Good Law. He thought the other Buddhist sects had missed the true way. The implicit patriotism of this sect is seen in its three vows: "I will be a pillar of Japan; I will be eyes to Japan; I will be a great ship for Japan." The contemporary militant _Soka Gakkai_ movement is a revival of the Nichiren sect, even to the constant repetition of the _daimoku_ formula: _Namu Myoho Renge Kyo,_ "Hail to the Lotus of the Good Law."

_____

_____

3. On a superficial view, direct or indirect or circumstantial evidence would appear to be distinct species of evidence; whereas these words denote only the different modes in which those classes of evidentiary facts are adduced to produce conviction. Circumstantial evidence is of a nature identically the same with direct evidence; the distinction is that by direct evidence is intended evidence that applied directly to the fact which forms the subject of inquiry, the *factum probandum;* circumstantial evidence is equally direct in its nature, but, as the name imports, is a direct evidence of minor fact or facts of such a nature that the mind is led into intuitively, or by a conscious process of reasoning, toward or to the conviction that from it or them some other fact may be inferred. A witness disposes that he saw A inflict on B a wound of which he instantly dies; this is a case of direct evidence. B dies of poisoning; A is proved to have had malice and other threats against him, and to have clandestinely purchased poison, wrapped in a particular paper, and of the same kind as that which has caused death. The paper is found in his secret drawer, and the poison gone. The evidence of these facts is direct; the facts themselves constitute indirect and circumstantial evidence as applicable to the inquiry whether a murder has been committed, and whether it was committed by A.

4. Mathematically, a worm is difficult to distinguish from a virus, and a communications network cannot be distinguished from the "network" formed by the busses inside a computer (unless the network includes workstations with independent processing capability, such as microcomputers). Colloquially, a virus alters other "programs," and a worm does not; however, mathematically the environment (sequence of bits in the address space) in which a worm moves is a "program." A virus does not propagate by itself, and it modifies other programs; the lack of independence may offer a mathematically definable difference between virus and worm. The physical implementation of a network implies very different countermeasures for a worm than for a virus.

---

5. For income tax reporting, firms generally use the Accelerated Cost Recovery System (ACRS), which specifies depreciation charges accelerated in three distinct ways. First, the depreciable lives themselves are generally shorter than economic lives. (Straight-line depreciation for a shorter period will produce depreciation charges accelerated when compared to straight-line over a longer period.) Second, for assets other than buildings, ACRS provides for depreciation over the specified life based on the 150-percent and 200-percent declining-balance depreciation method, which is more rapid than straight-line. ACRS assumes, however, that each asset is acquired at midyear of the year of acquisition, so the first-year percentage represents only a half-year of depreciation. Third, ACRS allows the entire depreciable basis to be written off over the depreciation period; salvage value is ignored.

These approaches to scientific texts should save you time, decrease your frustration, and improve your retention. If there were some magical way of putting a math book underneath your pillow at night, going to sleep and waking up with a full knowledge of the text, believe me, we'd be the first to show you. But there isn't. You just have to tough through these texts, using the techniques above. You should see a dramatic improvement in your understanding of these materials, and at the same time, an increase in speed.

Read the following passage and list the important facts in the margins. Be careful to exclude secondary facts that may be interesting but are not related or important to the main idea.

About 30,000 years ago Neanderthal man disappeared, displaced by *Homo sapiens*, a taller, slimmer, altogether agile and more handsome—at least to our eyes—race of people who arose in Africa 10,000 years ago, spread to the Near East, and then were drawn to Europe by the retreating ice sheets of the last great Ice Age. These were the Cro-Magnon people, who were responsible for the famous cave paintings at Lascaux in France and Altamira in Spain— the earliest signs of civilization in Europe, the work of the world's first artists. Although this was an immensely long time ago—some 20,000 years before the domestication of animals and the rise of farming—these Cro-Magnon people were identical to us: They had the same physique, the same brain, the same looks. And, unlike all previous hominids that roamed the earth, they could choke on food.

That may seem a trifling point, but the slight evolutionary change that pushed man's larynx deeper into his throat, and thus made choking a possibility, also brought with it the possibility of sophisticated, well-articulated speech. Other mammals have no contact between their airways and their esophagi. They can breathe and swallow at the same time, and there is no possibility of food going down the wrong way. But with *Homo sapiens,* food and drink must pass over the larynx on the way to the gullet and thus there is a constant risk that some will be inadvertently inhaled. In modern humans, the lowered larynx isn't in position from birth. It descends sometime between the ages of three and five months—curiously, the precise period when babies are likely to suffer from Sudden Infant Death Syndrome. At all events, the descended larynx explains why you can speak and your dog cannot.

According to studies conducted by Philip Lieberman at Brown University, Neanderthal man was physiologically precluded from uttering certain basic sounds such as the /e/ sound of *bee* or the /oo/ sound of *boot*. His speech, if it existed at all, would have been nasal-sounding and fairly imprecise—and that would have no doubt have greatly impeded his development.

It was long supposed that Neanderthal man was absorbed by the more advanced *Homo sapiens.* But recent evidence indicates that *Homo sapiens* and Neanderthals coexisted in the Near East for 30,000 years without interbreeding—strong evidence that the Neanderthals must have been a different species. It is interesting to speculate what would have become of these people had they survived. Would we have used them for slaves? For sport? Who can say?

At all events, Neanderthal man was hopelessly outclassed. Not only did *Homo sapiens* engage in art of astonishingly high quality, but they evinced other cultural achievements of a comparatively high order. They devised more specialized tools for a wider variety of tasks, and they hunted in a far more systematic and cooperative way. Whereas the food debris of the Neanderthals shows a wide variety of animal bones, suggesting that they took whatever they could find, archaeological remnants from *Homo sapiens* show that they sought out particular kinds of game and tracked animals seasonally. All of this strongly suggests that they possessed a linguistic system sufficiently sophisticated to deal with concepts such as "Today let's kill some red deer. You take some big sticks and drive the deer out of the woods and we'll stand by the riverbank with our spears and kill them as they come toward us." By comparison, Neanderthal speech may have been something more like "I'm hungry. Let's hunt." It may be no more than intriguing coincidence, but the area of Cro-Magnon's cave paintings is also the area containing Europe's oldest and most mysterious ethnic group, the Basques. Their language, called Euskara by its speakers, may be the last surviving remnant of the Neolithic languages spoken in Stone Age Europe and later displaced by Indo-European tongues. No one can say. What is certain is that Basque was already old by the time the Celts came to the region. Today it is the native tongue of about 600,000 people in Spain and 100,000 in France in an area around the Bay of Biscay stretching roughly from Bilbao to Bayonne and inland over the Pyrenees to Pamplona. Its remoteness from Indo-European is indicated by its words for the numbers one to five: *bat, bi, hirur, laur, bortz.* Many authorities believe there is simply no connection between Basque and any other known language.

Things to Take with You

Reading science texts depends on using techniques to keep you focused on the text. We all know that most of this information is dense, difficult to get through, and confusing. But the best readers give themselves a fighting chance by reading with their pens, by tracing main ideas and picking out important details. They use pictures, subheadings, translation, and derive the meaning of words in context. They don't try to memorize everything—they try to understand everything, giving themselves the best chance of remembering the important stuff.

Reading Zone 6

Read the following passage, marking in the margins your understanding of the larger issues, the important parts of each passage, and the facts that you think will be useful. There will be questions following the passage. *Do not time yourself.* When you start worrying about whipping through textbook material, you're missing the point. You can check your answers on page 242.

The concept of energy appears throughout every area of physics, and yet it is difficult to define in a general way just what energy is. Energy plays a central role in one of the fundamental natural laws called *conservation laws,* and looking at this role is as good a way as any to approach the question of what energy is. A conservation law always concerns a transformation or an interaction that occurs within some physical system or in a system and its surroundings. Some quantities that describe the state or condition of the system and surroundings may change during the transformation or interaction, but there may be one or more quantities that remain constant or are *conserved.* A familiar example is conservation of mass in chemical reactions. It has been established by a very large amount of experimental evidence that the total mass of the reactants in a chemical reaction is always equal to the total mass of all the products of the reaction. That is, the total mass is always the same after the reaction occurs as before. This generalization is called the principle of *conservation of mass,* and it is obeyed in all chemical reactions.

Something similar happens in collisions between bodies. For a body of mass m moving with speed v, we can define a quantity $\frac{1}{2}mv^2$, which we call the *kinetic energy* of the body. When two highly elastic or "springy" bodies (such as two hard steel ball bearings) collide, we find that the individual speeds change but that the total kinetic energy (the sum of the $\frac{1}{2}mv^2$ quantities for all the colliding bodies) is the same after the collision as before. We say that kinetic energy is *conserved* in such collisions. This result doesn't tell us what kinetic energy *is,* but only that it is useful in representing a conservation principle in certain kinds of interactions.

When two soft, deformable bodies, such as two balls of putty or chewing gum, collide, experiment shows that kinetic energy is *not* conserved. However, something else happens; the bodies become *warmer.* Furthermore, it turns out to be possible to work out a definite relationship between the temperature rise of the material and the loss of kinetic energy. We can define a new quantity, which we may call *internal energy,* that increases with temperature in a definite way, so that the *sum* of kinetic energy and internal energy *is* conserved in these collisions.

The significant discovery here is that it is possible to extend the principle of conservation of energy to a broader class of phenomena by defining a new form of energy. This is precisely how the principle has developed. Whenever an interaction has been studied in which it seems that the total energy in all known forms is *not* conserved, it has been found possible to define a new form of energy so that the *total* energy, including the new form, is conserved. These new forms have included energy associated with heat, with elastic deformations, with electric and mag-netic fields, and, in relativity theory, even with mass itself. Conservation of energy has the status, along with a small number of partners, of a *universal* conservation principle; no exception to its validity has ever been found.

1. The main question addressed by the passage is
   (A) What is conservation of energy?
   (B) What is an elastic deformation?
   (C) What is internal energy?
   (D) What happens in collisions between bodies?
   (E) What is energy?

2. Conservation of energy, as described in the passage, is exhibited in
   (A) two ball bearings colliding
   (B) reducing the speed of your car
   (C) turning off lights when not in use
   (D) resting after exercise
   (E) the conservation of mass in chemical reactions

3. Conservation of mass is mentioned in the passage because
   (A) chemistry and physics are related disciplines
   (B) chemistry is a sub-category of physics
   (C) it is the same as conservation of energy
   (D) it is a concept in chemistry that is similar to the conservation of energy in physics
   (E) it is necessary for an understanding of work and energy in physics

4. If a car were to slam into a large mound of wet clay, a probable result would be
   (A) a loss of energy
   (B) a loss of mass
   (C) a preservation of kinetic energy
   (D) a deformation of mass energy
   (E) a rise in clay temperature

5. In the passage, the term "elastic" means
   (A) steep
   (B) pliable
   (C) able to be stretched
   (D) hard and springy
   (E) heavy

Reflection

For any question you got wrong, go back and leave notes next to each answer choice indicating why it is correct or incorrect. It's important that you not only practice, but also reflect on your performance! This way, you'll see what issues give you trouble and gain a better understanding of how to improve.

Chapter 6 Summary

- Science texts are notoriously difficult (or thought to be difficult) because they tend to contain more technical language and are dense with information. However, having a plan of attack and employing a few basic reading strategies will get you far.

- Use a pencil or pencil to underline or circle key words and phrases that point to the main idea of the text. Don't just passively read the words on the page.

- Apply the pre-reading technique. If you're reading a textbook, for example, read the chapter or section headings or end-of-chapter questions. These will provide clues about a chapter's most important ideas.

- Be an active reader. Take notes or summarize each paragraph in the margins as you read.

- Pay attention to context to figure out the meaning of unfamiliar vocabulary. This is often more efficient than looking up the definition of every word you don't know, which can make you lose your focus.

- Translate technical terms and concepts into everyday, straightforward language.

CHAPTER 7

Social Sciences

"History will be kind to me, for I intend to write it."

—Winston Churchill

Tackling Social Science Texts

Not all required reading is in the natural sciences (thank goodness). Project reports, psychology, history, philosophy, and other social sciences all contain information you need to understand a discipline, but they usually aren't so terminology- or number-heavy. You need a different approach for this kind of reading, because it's just as important to keep your comprehension rates up here. "Who does not learn from history is doomed to repeat it," said George Santayana, and by the same token, whoever does not learn from history textbooks is doomed to repeat history class. In the social sciences, history, sociology, literature, psychology, and others, many of the textbooks will argue points of view. The first thing you should do is look at the title. Does it argue a point, or state a fact? If a book is called *Capitalist Patriarchy and the Case for Socialist Feminism*, you can have a pretty clear idea that the book will involve an intersection between economic and feminist issues. It is less clear what the book will be about if the title is *The American Revolution*.

Exercise 7

Look at the following titles and note whether the title is helpful or not helpful in identifying what the author's argument or point of view might be. You can check your answers on page 243.

1. *Financial Accounting for Beginners*

2. *Vietnam: The Untold Story of Government Corruption*

3. *From Fish to Man: Evolution's Progress*

4. *Russia's Quiet Threat*

5. *America the Beautiful*

6. *Society and Social Structures*

7. *Myths of Gender*

8. *Why I Kill: A Psychological Study*

9. *Parents and Children: The Communication Gap*

10. *The Evolution of Nuclear Strategy*

11. *Zen and the Art of Motorcycle Maintenance*

12. *Advanced Pascal*

13. *On Becoming a Novelist*

14. *Reading Smart*

15. *Information, Incentives, and Bargaining in the Japanese Economy*

The point is to use all the clues any book has to offer. In particular, any text that argues a point of view offers you a great advantage: There will be a linear discussion which will lead you to a conclusion, often stated in the opening chapter. Reading with your pen or pencil is essential in cases like this. Mark up the first and last chapters ruthlessly; if an author makes an argument the focus of an entire book, you must keep that argument in mind the whole time you read the book. It would be like playing baseball without knowing the goal of the game. You would know all of these facts, but have no idea how they relate to each other. You are more likely to remember them if you know that the goal of the game is to score the most runs by the end of the ninth inning.

Trace the Theme

Each paragraph will further the argument and back it up, or refute other arguments. Using your pen, you can quickly identify the main theme of the book and then trace that theme in the margin of your text. If the first paragraph says "Revolution is a good thing," then you should look for how the next paragraphs support or illuminate that statement by taking notes and underlining text. When you are done, you will have a complete outline of the text.

Separate the Facts

Once you understand what the larger endeavor is, you should distinguish primary facts from secondary facts. **Primary facts** are dates, names, and equations without which you couldn't begin to discuss the subject. **Secondary facts** are interesting but non-necessary information about the event. If the subject were the American Revolution, then 1776, George Washington, and the Boston Tea Party would be primary facts, as they are critical to any discussion of the American Revolution. The precise number of troops in Boston Harbor, the amount of the tea tax, and the age of King George III of England are all interesting and related to the discussion, but the American Revolution can be discussed without knowing any of them. They should be treated as secondary facts.

If this seems arbitrary, just ask yourself, "Can I talk about this subject completely without using these facts?" Don't confuse little stuff with more important larger issues—see how the facts relate to the main idea of the book. Once you've caught that magic thread of the main idea, the important facts seem to leap out at you.

Primary vs. Secondary Facts

The best way to tell if a fact is primary or secondary is to pare an event down to its simplest scenario, and then keep adding until you get to the level of information that describes the subject in sufficient detail.

Let's take the American Revolution (again). Start with the basics:

1. There was a conflict.

   This doesn't fully capture the subject. So expand.

2. There was a conflict between the colonies (America) and the empire (Britain).

   Still, more is needed.

3. There was an 18th-century conflict between the colonies (America) and the empire (Britain) which came to a head over the "taxation without representation" issue. America's army was led by General George Washington, who later became the first president of the United States. Great Britain was led (through not militarily) by King George III. America won.

This is enough to get a fair idea of the subject, and to go much further gets into secondary facts. Tailor your expansion to the subject. You may want to have a larger group of primary facts to describe World War I than you would use to describe your local dogcatcher elections.

Things to Take with You

Just as with scientific texts, reading social science texts efficiently requires you to employ strategies that keep you focused on the text and reading task at hand. Use context clues, trace the theme, and distinguish between primary and secondary facts. Staying engaged is also key: Take notes in the margins, underline, highlight, or even draw pictures if doing so will help you remember important concepts and keep your focus. Remember, don't try to *memorize* everything; try to *understand* everything.

Reading Zone 7

Read the next passage, pre-reading subheadings and the questions. You can check your answers to the multiple-choice questions on page 243.

THE DUTCH IN INDONESIA

The saga of the Dutch in Indonesia began in 1596, when four small Dutch vessels led by the incompetent and arrogant Cornelius de Houtman anchored in the roads of Banten, then the largest pepper port in the archipelago. Repeatedly blown off course and racked by disease and dissension, the Houtman expedition had been a disaster from the start. In Banten, the sea-weary Dutch crew went on a drinking binge and had to be chased back to their ships by order of an angry prince, who then refused to do business with such unruly *farang*. Hopping from port to port down the north coast of Java, de Houtman wisely confined his sailors to their ships and managed to purchase some spices. But on arriving in Bali, the entire crew jumped ship and it was some months before de Houtman could muster a quorum for returning to voyage.

Arriving back in Holland in 1597 after an absence of two years, with only three lightly laden ships and a third of their crew, the de Houtman voyage was nonetheless hailed as a success. So dear were spices in Europe at this time, that the sale of the meager cargoes sufficed to cover all expenses and even produced a modest profit for the investors! This touched off a veritable fever of speculation in Dutch commercial circles, and in the following year five consortiums dispatched a total of 22 ships to the Indies.

The Dutch East India Company

The Netherlands was at this time rapidly becoming the commercial centre of Northern Europe. Since the fifteenth century, ports of the two Dutch coastal provinces, Holland and Zeeland, had served as entrepots for goods shipped to Germany and the Baltic states. Many Dutch merchants grew wealthy on this carrying trade, and following the outbreak of war with Spain in 1568, they began to expand their shipping fleets rapidly, so that by the 1590s they were trading directly with Levant and Brazil.

Thus when a Dutchman published his itinerary to the East Indies in 1595–1596, it occasioned the immediate dispatch of the de Houtman and later expeditions. Indeed, so keen was the interest in direct trade with the Indies, that all Dutch traders soon came to recognize the need for cooperation—to minimize competition and maximize profits. In 1602, therefore, they formed the United Dutch East India Company (known by its Dutch initials VOC), one of the first joint-stock corporations in history. It was capitalized at more than six million guilders and empowered by the states-general to negotiate treaties, raise armies, build fortresses, and wage war on behalf of the Netherlands in Asia.

The VOC's whole purpose and philosophy can be summed up in a single word—monopoly. Like the Portuguese before them, the Dutch dreamed of securing absolute control of the East Indies spice trade, which traditionally had passed through many Muslim and Mediterranean hands. The profits from such a trade were potentially enormous, in the order of several thousand percent.

In its early years, the VOC met with only limited success. Several trading posts were opened, and Ambon was taken from the Portuguese (in 1605), but Spanish and English, not to mention Muslim, competition kept spice prices high in Indonesia and low in Europe. Then in 1614, a young accountant by the name of Jan Pietieszoon Coen convinced the directors that only a more forceful policy would make the company profitable. Coen was given command of VOC operations, and promptly embarked on a series of military adventures that were to set the pattern for Dutch behavior in the region.

The Founding of Batavia

Coen's first step was to establish a permanent headquarters at Jayakarta on the northwestern coast of Java, close to the pepper-producing parts of Sumatra and the strategic Sundra Straits. In 1618, he sought and received permission from Prince Wijayakrama of Jayakarta to expand the existing Dutch post, and proceeded to throw up a stone barricade mounted with cannon. The prince protested that fortifications were not provided for in their agreement and Coen responded by bombarding the palace, thereby reducing it to rubble. A siege of the fledgling Dutch fortress ensued, in which the powerful Bantenese and a recently arrived English fleet joined the Jayakartans. Coen was not so easily beaten, however (his motto: "Never Despair!"), and escaped to Amboton leaving a handful of his men in defense of the fort and its valuable contents.

Five months later, Coen returned to discover his men still in possession of their post. Though outnumbered 30-to-1 they had rather unwittingly played one foe against another by acceding to any and all demands, but were never actually required to surrender their position due to the mutual suspicion and timidity of the three attacking parties. Coen set his adversaries to flight in a series of dramatic attacks, undertaken with a small force of 1,000 men that included several score of fearsome Japanese mercenaries. The town of Jayakarta was razed to the ground and construction of a new Dutch town begun, eventually to include canals, drawbridges, docks, warehouses, barracks, a central square, a city hall, and a church—all protected by a high stone wall and a moat—a copy, in short, of Amsterdam itself.

The only sour note in the proceedings was struck by the revelation that during the darkest days of the siege, many of the Dutch defenders had behaved themselves in a most unseemly manner—drinking, singing, and fornicating for several nights in succession. Worst of all, they had broken open the company storehouse and divided the contents up amongst themselves. Coen, a strict disciplinarian, ordered the immediate execution of those involved, and memories of the infamous siege soon faded—save one. The defenders had dubbed their fortress "Batavia," and the new name stuck.

Coen's next step was to secure control of the five tiny nutmeg- and mace-producing Banda Islands. In 1621, he led an expeditionary force there and within a few weeks rounded up and killed most of the 15,000 inhabitants on the island. Three of the islands were then transformed into spice plantations managed by Dutch colonists and worked by slaves.

In the years that followed, the Dutch gradually tightened their grip on the spice trade. From their base at Ambon, they attempted to "negotiate" a monopoly in cloves with the rulers of Ternaate and Tidore. But "leakages" continued to occur. Finally, in 1649, the Dutch began a series of yearly sweeps of the entire area. The infamous *hongi* (war-fleet) expeditions defended islands other than Ambon and Ceram, where the Dutch were firmly established. So successful were these expeditions, that half of the islanders starved for lack of trade, and the remaining half were reduced to abject poverty.

Still the smuggling of cloves and clove trees continued. Traders obtained these and other goods at the new Islamic port of Makassar, in southern Sulawesi. The Dutch repeatedly blockaded Makassar and imposed treaties theoretically barring the Makassarese from trading with other nations, but were unable for many years to enforce them. Finally, in 1669, following three years of bitter and bloody fighting, the Makassarese surrendered to superior Dutch and Buginese forces. The Dutch now placed their Bugis ally, Aarung Palakka, in charge of Makassar. The bloodletting did not stop here, however, for Arung Palakka embarked on a reign of terror to extend his control over all of southern Sulawesi.

The Dutch in Java

By such nefarious means the Dutch had achieved effective control of the eastern archipelago and its lucrative spice trade by the end of the seventeenth century. In the western half of the archipelago, however, they became increasingly embroiled in fruitless intrigues and wars, particularly on Java. This came about largely because the Dutch presence at Batavia disturbed a delicate balance of power on Java.

1. Cornelius de Houtman could be described as
   (A) a daring adventurer
   (B) the father of the spice trade
   (C) the first casualty of the Dutch in Indonesia
   (D) an ineffective commandant
   (E) an inspirational leader

2. The Dutch East India Company at first encountered
   (A) enormous success
   (B) limited success
   (C) limited failure
   (D) enormous failure
   (E) horrendous weather

3. The Dutch control of the spice trade in Java was achieved through
   (A) diplomatic negotiation
   (B) military conquest
   (C) sordid alliances
   (D) commerce and trade
   (E) correspondence and requisition

4. During the siege of Coen's position, his soldiers behaved
   (A) with military decorum
   (B) with vengeance and anger
   (C) with honor and discipline
   (D) with dipsomaniac fervor
   (E) until the fourth month of the siege

5. It can be inferred from the passage that the word "farang" means
   (A) friends
   (B) foreigners
   (C) Dutchmen
   (D) drunkards
   (E) sailors

Reflection

For any question you got wrong, go back and leave notes next to each answer choice indicating why it is correct or incorrect. It's important that you not only practice, but also reflect on your performance! This way, you'll see what issues give you trouble and gain a better understanding of how to improve.

Chapter 7 Summary

- Read social science texts just as you would any other text—that is, use strategies like pre-reading, and mark up the pages with notes, underlining, circling, and highlighting.

- Trace the theme in order to create an outline of the text.

- Separate primary facts from secondary facts. Primary facts are those which you absolutely need to know in order to understand or discuss a given subject. Secondary facts are interesting and often deepen your knowledge about a subject, but they're not essential.

- Don't try to memorize everything—it's impossible. Focus on understanding the text and having a solid grasp of its main ideas.

CHAPTER 8

Humanities

"The notion that every well educated person would have a mastery of at least the basic elements of the humanities, sciences, and social sciences is a far cry from the specialized education that most students today receive, particularly in the research universities."

—Joseph Stiglitz

What Are the "Humanities"?

What does the term "humanities" refer to? It depends on whom you ask, but if you are preparing for a test like the SAT, ACT, or MCAT, you know that some passages are not about science (natural or social), but rather deal with subjects of study like art, art history, literary criticism, music, philosophy, and so on. All of these disciplines are usually lumped into the broad category known as the "humanities."

Humanities courses are often required in college. These subjects train your brain in logic and emotional intelligence, as well as help you become a more well-rounded thinker. And this is perhaps the reason why passages related to humanities disciplines show up so often on standardized tests. Therefore, boosting your skills in this area is essential to test-taking strategy and survival. For example, you may or may not have majored in the history of dance, but you might get a passage on that topic. However, there is no reason to fear such a passage; for the most part, you don't need outside knowledge to work with humanities texts. You just need to translate what you find into easier language, and then use that knowledge to process the questions and answer choices.

Let us prove this to you. Start by reading the following passage:

> Graham's groundbreaking style grew from her experimentation with the elemental movements of contraction and release. By focusing on the basic activities of the human form, she enlivened the body with raw, electric emotion. The sharp, angular, and direct movements of her technique were a dramatic departure from the predominant style of the time.

So, how are you feeling? Are you worried that you must know the precise meaning of "contraction and release"? That you should be able to list the basic activities of the human form? (Are there three of them? Twenty-nine?) That you should know what the "predominant style of the time" was? If so, take three deep breaths, and then keep reading.

You don't need to know any of this. Here is what test writers can reasonably expect of you: that you understand that Graham was new, innovative, groundbreaking—or some other word that means original. You should understand that she focused on the human form and body. Finally, you should recognize that if her technique was sharp, angular, and direct, it's fair to ask you to also know that the style of her time was *not* sharp, *not* angular, and *not* direct. (The text says that she was doing new stuff, right?) And that's it.

Cards Against the Humanities

So, let's look at some humanities paragraphs and practice translating them into easier, everyday language. We've done the first one for you, based on the previous passage. You can check your answers to the three examples on page 244.

Card 8.1

Scary humanities text:

Graham's groundbreaking style grew from her experimentation with the elemental movements of contraction and release. By focusing on the basic activities of the human form, she enlivened the body with raw, electric emotion. The sharp, angular, and direct movements of her technique were a dramatic departure from the predominant style of the time.

Details you may be worrying about, but shouldn't:

What are contraction and release? What are the basic activities of the human form? What was the predominant style of the time?

Translation:

Graham made a new style by doing totally new stuff with the body.

Card 8.2

Scary humanities text:

If postmodernism were simply a period, it would be reasonable to search for its origins in earlier times and to understand it as a reaction to and/or a refinement of aesthetic ideas of previous periods. But postmodernism taken as an attitude suggests ways listeners of today can understand music of various eras. It is in the minds of today's listeners, more than in history, that we find clues to the sources of postmodernism. It comes from the present—from ourselves—more than from the past. Music has become postmodern as we, its late twentieth-century listeners, have become postmodern.

Details you may be worrying about, but shouldn't:

What is postmodernism?

Translation:

_____

_____

_____

Card 8.3

Scary humanities text:

It is with Hegel, however, that the modern notion of dialectic crystallized. While his thinking was shaped by Kant's discussion of antimonies in *The Critique of Pure Reason,* Hegel considered dialectic a medium of truth rather than a means to uncover illusion. Above all, Hegel's dialectic was based on his emphatic belief in connectedness, or the interrelation of all aspects of the universe.

Details you may be worrying about, but shouldn't:

Who are Hegel and Kant? What was the ancient notion of dialectic? What the heck are "antimonies"?

Translation:

_____

_____

_____

Card 8.4

Scary humanities text:

George Wellwarth discusses Beckett's concept of a protean reality: "What all these things—the sameness of human beings and their actions, the vanity of human ambition, the useless-ness of thought—amount to is a pessimism deeper than any that has ever been put into words before. Throughout Beckett's work we can find evidence of his conviction that everything is hopeless, meaningless, purposeless, and, above all, agonizing to endure. Beckett's people are leveled off and merged into each other by being all more or less physically disabled—as if this were really the common condition on earth. . . . Beckett is a prophet of negation and sterility. He holds out no hope to humanity, only a picture of unrelieved blackness; and those who profess to see in Beckett signs of a Christian approach or signs of compassion are simply refusing to see what is there." Perhaps Beckett himself stated his dilemma most succinctly in *L'Innommable*: "Dans ma vie, puisqu'il faut l'appeler ainsi, il y eut trois choses, l'impossibilité de parler, l'impossibilité de me taire, et la solitude." ("One must speak; man cannot possibly communicate with his fellows, but the alternative—silence—is irreconcilable with human existence.")

Details you may be worrying about, but shouldn't:

Who exactly are these two people? I don't read French.

Translation:

_____

_____

_____

How did that go? Are you feeling more confident about the ability to translate seemingly difficult ideas into simpler language? We hope so. Of course, we don't want you to think that difficult texts are always "really" about a totally simple idea. If that were true, writers would usually just write using the simple ideas. As you become more adept at reading in the humanities, you will be able to make even more sense of the details that we are telling you not to worry about just now. And it is worth learning to read better (and smarter). Of course, you already believe that; this is why you are here.

Reading Zone 8

Read the next passage, using pre-reading and the questions as guidelines for reading the passage. You'll find your speed improves as you can disregard the information that you already know you won't need. Still, don't time yourself—you shouldn't be concerned with speed through textbooks yet. This is a long passage, so pre-reading is very important. You can check your answers to the questions on page 244.

> Gauguin left France on 3 July 1895, never to return. He had presided over a failed sale of his earlier work and had left the majority of his paintings in the hands of at least two obscure men, Auguste Bauchy and Georges Chaudet. Together with his literary agent Charles Morice, his faithful friend Daniel de Manfried, and later, Ambroise Vollard, his dealer, these men kept Gauguin informed about his business affairs in France and made it possible for him to enjoy periods of prosperity amid bouts of depression, illness, and poverty. Because they oversaw Gauguin's financial well-being from afar, the many letters he wrote to them are full of information about financial matters and the state of his health. When these letters are read as an ensemble, his life sounds more miserable than it was, and almost masks the brilliant paintings, drawings, and prints that survive him.

During the eight years that elapsed between Gauguin's final departure from France and his death on the distant island of Hiva Oa in the Marquesas, he was in the hospital at least four times, often for prolonged periods; claimed to have attempted suicide once and perhaps succumbed to its temptations in 1903; built three houses; fathered at least three children; edited one newspaper and wrote, designed, and printed another; completed three book-length texts; sent paintings and drawings to many European exhibitions; finished nearly 100 paintings; made over 400 woodcuts; carved scores of pieces of wood; wrote nearly 150 letters; and fought both civil and ecclesiastical authorities with all the gusto of a youth. He was only fifty-four years old when he died, but he had lived his life with such fervor and worked so hard when he was healthy that we must remember the achievements even as we read the litany of the failures and miseries in the chronology.

Unfortunately, none of the great monographic exhibitions devoted to Gauguin since his death has done justice to this extraordinary phase in his working life. By the time the French organizers of the 1906 exhibition had begun their work, a good many of the most important paintings had already left France for private collections in Russia and Germany. Indeed, without the paintings bought by Karl Ernst Osthaus, Sergei Shchukin, and Ivan Morosov, it is difficult to understand the late Gauguin fully, and many of these paintings were not in France to be loaned to the 1906 Gauguin exhibition. Only the 1903 exhibition held in Vollard's gallery a few months after Gauguin's death had a generous enough selection of major paintings and transfer drawings to give full measure to the achievement of the artist in his last years. Yet even this large exhibition was insufficient for a full understanding of his oeuvre from 1896 to 1903 because it contained almost exclusively works made in the last three years of his life.

There are several important ways in which Gauguin's oeuvre from the last Polynesian period can be differentiated from that of the first. During the first trip, Gauguin's work took two different directions, both of which were recognized by critics of the 1893 exhibition. First, he represented scenes of daily life just as his hero, Delacroix, had done in Morocco; second, he created idealized illustrations of Polynesian tales of religious and mythical events about which he read. Both these enterprises were characterized by a sort of ethnographic focus on Tahiti before its colonialization. Indeed, hints of the colonial presence are so rare in the paintings that, even when they do exist, one must be sensitized to recognize them.

Neither of these ethnographic concerns was so evident in Gauguin's work of the last Polynesian period. Indeed, Gauguin returned to Tahiti with his mind full of new ideas about comparative religion, politics, and social philosophy. He also took with him an even larger stock of photographs and reproductions of other works of art than he had in the years 1891 to 1893, and, as many scholars have pointed out, he made considerable use of this material. Two of the photographs often referred to were of the Javanese temple of Borobudur.

The Tahiti to which Gauguin returned in 1895 had become even more colonial in the two years since he had left, and there is little doubt that Gauguin disliked most of the "progress" that he saw. Yet we must also remember that Tahiti had changed in those years perhaps less than Gauguin himself had, and that given his earlier experience, the painter could have predicted what he was going to find on his return. His late paintings, traced and transferred drawings, and sculpture lack the vivid directness of the work from his earlier, ethnographic phase. In these years, he was more interested in the creation of works of art that transcended the particular place in which they were made. His late work is more obviously mediated than the earlier, and he created works of art as if to decorate a new mythic universe. His overt worldliness, his conflation of religious traditions of East, West, and Oceania, of ancient and modern, must have seemed strange to the majority of Eurocentric Parisians for whom his art was made. Today, in an age of rampant international capitalism, his world view is easier to find relevant and even important.

1. From 1895 to 1903, Gauguin's artistic activity can best be described as
   - (A) impoverished
   - (B) alien
   - (C) ethnographic
   - (D) frenzied
   - (E) transcendental

2. It can be inferred from the passage that the word "oeuvre" means
   - (A) style
   - (B) area of obsession
   - (C) overtness
   - (D) work
   - (E) openness

3. Which of the following statements is best supported by the passage?
   - (A) Paul Gauguin was impressed by the physical beauty of Tahiti.
   - (B) Paul Gauguin believed in civil reform.
   - (C) Paul Gauguin committed suicide.
   - (D) Paul Gauguin was not confined to one area of expression.
   - (E) Paul Gauguin, in his later years, abandoned Europe due to religious pressure.

4. Paul Gauguin's later work was
   - (A) obsessively involved in ethnography
   - (B) casually informed by ethnography
   - (C) revered in Europe
   - (D) informed by philosophical issues
   - (E) imitative of Javanese life

5. Gauguin's exhibition of 1893 was marked by
   (A) scenes from daily life
   (B) ideas of comparative religion, politics, and social philosophy
   (C) the lack of the vivid directness of earlier work
   (D) photographs of the Javanese temple of Borobudur
   (E) an abandonment of the island of Hiva Oa as a subject

Reflection

For any question you got wrong, go back and leave notes next to each answer choice indicating why it is correct or incorrect. It's important that you not only practice, but also reflect on your performance! This way, you'll see what issues give you trouble and gain a better understanding of how to improve.

Chapter 8 Summary

- The "humanities" is a broad category referring to disciplines like art, literature, philosophy, and music.

- Humanities courses are often required in college, and passages related to humanities subjects happen to be a favorite of test writers. Therefore, knowing how to read a humanities-related passage is essential to your test-taking survival.

- Even if you're not familiar with a particular topic, use the context to figure out the meaning of the text.

- Translate technical terms and concepts into everyday, straightforward language.

CHAPTER 9

Fiction: Part 1

"Reading fiction is important. It is a vital means of imagining a life other than our own, which in turn makes us more empathetic beings. Following complex story lines stretches our brains beyond the 140 characters of sound-bite thinking, and staying within the world of a novel gives us the ability to be quiet and alone, two skills that are disappearing faster than the polar icecaps."

—Ann Patchett

Why Fiction?

The way we first learn to read is through stories, and the way we first learn about people, about anyone outside ourselves and our friends and our family, is through fiction. If you're reading books for leisure, for school, or for work—it doesn't matter. You're trying to learn something and be entertained at the same time. In a Sherlock Holmes novel, you're trying to figure out "whodunit" and how. In an Isaac Asimov novel, you're trying to imagine his created universe, and how it resembles your own. Sometimes the struggle is less visible. Sometimes all the author offers you is a little slice of life—a view into someone else's world that may be as clouded as your own.

The reason we're talking about what fiction does is that the first question you have to ask yourself about a work of fiction is: What do I need it for? It will be rare that you will read a textbook only for fun. A journalistic piece will inform you and entertain you, but it is not a commitment like a novel or a collection of short stories. Reading fiction for leisure and reading it for school are completely different experiences. We'll go into why and how you should read for each purpose in a second, but you should be aware of why you are reading each book. A book discussion in a classroom is very different than how you might talk about a book with a friend at a party. If you and a friend are grabbing handfuls of chips at a social gathering, and you start spouting off about the "post-modernist anagrammatical games in *Lolita*, and the ubiquitous self-referencing aspect visible once one knots symbolism and linguistic play," your friend will either leave, be bored to tears, or will slug you (and well she should) for your turning what used to be an interesting novel to read into a dull literary exercise. When you read books for pleasure, lighten up. It's good to notice the scholarly stuff—but that isn't the point when reading for pleasure.

Have a Plan

A little general strategy never hurts. Have a plan before you pick up a book. Don't intend to sit down and read the whole thing in one sitting. If you love the book, and your reading is going fine, then go beyond what you've planned. But when you pick up a book, you should read it every day until you are done, even if you can only devote fifteen minutes a day to it. Set a goal of ten days for every book. If you can't reach that goal, finish as fast as you can. Why? The more you set stuff aside, the less you remember about earlier stuff. The book loses all of its momentum. The characters, which once seemed real, now seem flat, like soda with the cap left off. Think of it as a commitment. If a book has fifteen chapters, break it up into three-chapter segments. Tell yourself you're going to read a segment today, two tomorrow, and one segment each day until you finish it. If you fall behind, you stand a much greater chance of not finishing the book or losing track of the events, characters, and language. Plan your reading before you pick up the book—then you can determine how you're doing.

Reading Fiction for School

Oh boy, another assignment. You figure, hey, it's fiction. No problem. You struggle through it, slowly, searching word by word, and it's a chore. More than a chore. It's the worst thing in the world. And yet, had you picked up the same book to read for leisure, chances are good that it would have been a more enjoyable experience. What is this event called "assigned reading" that drives people up a tree? A student once said that if eating chocolate was required, everyone would all of a sudden hate chocolate. While you may disagree with that specific example, the idea that an "assignment = back-breaking chore" is worth examining.

How do you keep your head in the book? For starters, learn about the author. Most novels will have an About the Author blurb, which is usually at the back of the book. Read it. If it's not there, look at the first few pages. The more you know about an author, the more interested you become in his or her work. Sometimes authors' lives are even more fascinating than their books (don't let a teacher hear you say that, though). But the best information helps make the author's work more lively for you. Virginia Woolf, a famous British author (*To the Lighthouse, A Room of One's Own, Orlando,* and so on), suffered from bouts of depression and often experienced delirious visions, and in spite of all this, she produced some of the most complicated, inventive work in the English language. Knowing biographical details can often illuminate a work and help you understand certain artistic choices or themes that you otherwise may not have.

How Does It Start?

Next, look at the title and any quotes the author has chosen to introduce their work—keeping in mind you are doing all this before you open up to the first page of the book. For example, Ernest Hemingway wrote a book called *The Sun Also Rises.* He introduces it with two quotations. First, one from Gertrude Stein, a writer who was seen as an oracle for the writers of the twenties in Paris. "You are a lost generation," she says. You want to keep that in mind when you read this book. The novel is set in the post-World War I era, when many people lost their belief in anything. The second quotation is one from a book of the Bible, from Ecclesiastes, which explains the title of the book (look it up!). The point is, use all the clues provided for you. These are things to keep in your mind as you read the book—often they'll explain the weird things going on. The characters in *The Sun Also Rises* are all wounded in some way, all drunkards and all behave very badly. If you know that he's writing about a generation decimated by World War I, you might also sympathize a little more.

Big Picture, Small Picture

How is reading for school different than reading any other way? At first glance, it seems to be the exact same thing. Your eyes take in the information; your brain decodes it. But when you have to read for school, you have to remember what you've read (the details) and you have to see larger things the author is doing (symbols, plots, metaphor, etc.). Now, in a textbook, you would mark significant ideas in the margin. Would you do the same thing in a work of fiction? You bet. But you have to mark the things that are important to fiction, the symbols, plot, metaphor, and so on.

In your own mind, you have to get the action clear. That's the primary thing. If you don't know what's going on, you're going to have trouble seeing larger, hidden themes. Authors don't like to make everything as simple as they could (although the best authors do that and more). You have to keep track of what's going on. And where better than the margin of the book itself? At the end of each chapter, summarize the events of the chapter. If there are section breaks, you can do it there. We're just talking plot here. By plot, we mean what happens. That's it. For now, nothing else.

So you know what's going on. So what? Your teachers will expect you to know more: images, themes, the stuff that goes beyond the plot. You can do something called theme-marking. **Theme-marking** means keeping track of all instances of a single image or single character. Look for things which keep appearing. You don't have to know what it means. Just mark where it occurs. Let's look at an example: If a dove keeps appearing, make a mark where it appears. Then, after you're done reading the book, you can start to make connections about where that bird appears. It doesn't have to be the exact same thing—it can be a type of thing, like death images, or birth images, or a color. Maybe that bird appears just before the same type of scene happens. Maybe just after. But theme-marking makes it clear that something's going on. And as you read your book and you start to mark it up, the connection between those themes will become clearer.

Read the next passage, which is from a 1940 novel by Raymond Chandler. As you read, pay attention to the images the author uses and note them in the margins. Try to figure out how the images help you understand other literary devices like tone and characterization. Then, on a separate sheet of paper, write a summary of the passage.

> The car was a dark blue seven-passenger sedan, a Packard of the latest model, custom-built. It was the kind of car you wear your rope pearls in. It was parked by a fire-hydrant and a dark foreign-looking chauffeur with a face of carved wood was behind the wheel. The interior was upholstered in quilted grey chenille. The Indian put me in the back. Sitting there alone I felt like a high-class corpse, laid out by an undertaker with a lot of good taste.

The Indian got in beside the chauffeur and the car turned in the middle of the block and a cop across the street said: "Hey," weakly, as if he didn't mean it, and then bent down quickly to tie his shoe.

We went west, dropped over to Sunset and slid fast and noiseless along that. The Indian sat motionless beside the chauffeur. An occasional whiff of his personality drifted back to me. The driver looked as if he was half asleep but he passed the fast boys in the convertible sedans as though they were being towed. They turned on all the green lights for him. Some drivers are like that. He never missed one.

We curved through the bright mile or two of the Strip, past the antique shops with famous screen names on them, past the windows full of point lace and ancient pewter, past the gleaming new night clubs with famous chefs and equally famous gambling rooms, run by polished graduates of the Purple Gang, past the Georgian-Colonial vogue, now old hat, past the handsome modernistic buildings in which the Hollywood flesh-peddlers never stop talking money, past a drive-in lunch which somehow didn't belong, even though the girls wore white silk blouses and drum majorettes' shakos and nothing below the hips but glazed kid Hessian boots. Past all this and down a wide smooth curve to the bridle path of Beverly Hills and lights to the south. All colours of the spectrum and crystal clear in an evening without fog, past the shadowed mansions up on the hills to the north, past Beverly Hills altogether and up into the twisting foothill boulevard and the sudden cool dusk and the drift of wind from the sea.

It had been a warm afternoon, but the heat was gone. We whipped past a distant cluster of lighted buildings and an endless series of lighted mansions, not too close to the road. We dipped down to skirt a huge green polo field with another equally huge practice field beside it, soared again to the top of a hill and swing mountainward up a steel hill road of clean concrete that passed orange groves, some rich man's pet because this is not orange country, and then little by little the lighted windows of the millionaires' homes were gone and the road narrowed and this was Stillwood Heights.

The smell of sage drifted up from a canyon and made me think of a dead man and a moonless sky. Straggly stucco houses were moulded flat to the side of the hill, like bas-reliefs. Then there were no more houses, just the still dark foothills with an early star or two above them, and the concrete ribbon of road and a sheer drop on one side into a tangle of scrub oak and manzanita where sometimes you can hear the call of the quails if you stop and keep still and wait. On the other side of the road was a raw clay bank at the edge of which a few unbeatable wild flowers hung on like naughty children that won't go to bed.

Then the road twisted into a hairpin turn and the big tyres scratched over loose stones, and the car tore less soundlessly up a long driveway lined with the wild geraniums. At the top of this, faintly lighted, lonely as a light-house stood an eyrie, an eagle's nest, an angular building of stucco and glass brick, raw and modernistic and yet not ugly and altogether a swell place for a psychic consultant to hang out his shingle. Nobody would be able to hear any screams.

Piece Together the Puzzle

A summary of the passage could read:

> I got in a car with a chauffeur and an Indian, and drove through L.A. to a deserted spot in the hills.

If this were all there were to it, Chandler could have saved an awful lot of time and paper by just summarizing. Unlike journalism, the writing itself contains the point. Images and emotions are evoked while the plot develops—two for the price of one. There has to be a reason for these images. Chandler is no dummy. But it's not his job to explain them; it's your job to figure out why he chose what he did.

This process doesn't have to be a chore. View it as a puzzle, as a mystery you have to solve. All the pieces are in front of you, and the author's even given you hints how to assemble them. Look back at the story. Repeated images are of light and color. The street he travels on is called "sunset" and he travels from "light," to his destination which is "moonless." His journey from light to dark should give you the creeps. Something ominous is happening here—circling all the words about light and color will show you the progression.

Some other images should leap out at you from the passage. He lies in the backseat "like a corpse." He is reminded of a "dead man." There is "raw" clay and the car "twisted" and "tore." His final observation is that "[n]obody would be able to hear any screams." He feels like he's becoming part of death, that somehow, this meeting scares him to death. Look for the meaning in images, but start with identifying the images themselves. You'll find these images stay in your mind long after finishing the book.

The Mind's Eye

Why do we remember so much from fiction? I mean, we can read a two-hundred page textbook and only remember bolded headings and a few chapter titles, while we can read a two-hundred pile novel and remember nearly every scene in the book. What is unique to fiction?

It's not really about fiction—it's about the way humans are built. We all come with active imaginations. It's not just the ability to visualize things not present—research shows that most animals have that capability. First, it is the ability to piece together a whole out of incomplete information. For example, if you were on vacation in the Adirondacks and returned to your cabin to find large paw tracks covering the floor, claw marks on the walls, your bed torn to ribbons, and all your honey gone, you could reasonably imagine the bear that went through your stuff. Second, it is the ability to place yourself sensually (hearing, seeing, smelling) and emotionally in other places and other peoples' minds. For example, try to imagine the joy felt at defeating a dragon and saving the kingdom, or the frustration of being the dragon, defeated by a tiny mortal. Fiction releases those abilities, encourages us to use them. And so we remember. Because it makes us use a part of ourselves that we normally try to control. Face it—day-to-day existence is dull. We use our imaginations to escape that boredom, but we have to use it in small doses. If you're too caught up in your imagination while driving your car, the repair bills will be enormous. Fiction invites you to imagine all day long and get something out of it.

As a reader, you must exploit the power to imagine. When dialogue is spoken, you have to make an effort to hear it. When a landscape is described, you have to make an effort to see it. The best authors make it easy for you. Look at a John Steinbeck landscape, or listen to a Toni Morrison character speak. Once you make the leap from fiction being merely words on a page to concrete images and experiences, your retention will jump a level.

Think of a movie. Why do we frequently remember more from a movie (specific lines and images, for example) than we can from a book? Because, first of all, most of the way we deal with the world is visual. A movie is primarily a visual experience. Second, a movie has sound to reinforce the visual, providing another reason to remember. A movie plays to the way our mind works. If you can make a book do the same, you'll find your enjoyment of the book increases as well. Try to imagine it has a movie. Think of specific, visual images that bring the story to life.

This is a good moment to bring back one important idea. Remember how we said you had to be involved in your reading? Well, fiction is the real test. If you get involved and start using your own abilities when you read fiction, you'll rarely find yourself wondering where you are and what you are reading. Keep focused on the book—a high concentration level here reaps even higher rewards.

The following passage is from a work by Ernest Hemingway. Look for the visual clues that allow you to picture it. Try to get a feel for how the author describes the scene. Allow the visuals to help bring the story to life for you.

> At noon of Sunday, the 6th of July, the fiesta exploded. There is no other way to describe it. People had been coming in all day from the country, but they were assimilated in the town and you did not notice them. The square was as quiet in the hot sun as on any other day. The peasants were in the outlying wine-shops. There they were drinking, getting ready for the fiesta. They had come in so recently from the plains and the hills that it was necessary that they make their shifting in values gradually. They could not start in paying cafe prices. They got their money's

worth in the wine-shops. Money still had a definite value in hours worked and bushels of grain sold. Late in the fiesta it would not matter what they paid, nor where they bought.

Now on the day of the starting of the fiesta of San Fermin they had been in the wine-shops of the narrow streets of the town since early morning. Going down the streets in the morning on the way to mass in the cathedral, I heard them singing through the open doors of the shops. They were warming up. There were many people at the eleven o'clock mass. San Fermin is also a religious festival.

I walked down the hill from the cathedral and up the street to the cafe on the square. It was a little before noon. Robert Cohn and Bill were sitting at one of the tables. The marble-topped tables and the white wicker chairs were gone. They were replaced by cast-iron tables and severe folding chairs. The cafe was like a battleship stripped for action. Today the waiters did not leave you alone all morning to read without asking if you wanted to order something. A waiter came up as soon as I sat down.

"What are you drinking?" I asked Bill and Robert.

"Sherry," Cohn said.

"Jerez," I said to the waiter.

Before the waiter brought the sherry the rocket that announced the fiesta went up in the square. It burst and there was a gray ball of smoke high up above the Theatre Gayarre, across on the other side of the plaza. The ball of smoke hung in the sky like a shrapnel burst, and as I watched, another rocket came up to it, trickling smoke in the bright sunlight. I saw the bright flash as it burst and another little cloud of smoke appeared. By the time the second rocket had burst there were so many people in the arcade, that had been empty a minute before, that the waiter, holding the bottle high up over his head, could hardly get through the crowd to our table. People were coming into the square from all sides, and down the street we heard the pipes and the fifes and the shrill and the drums pounding, and behind them came the men and boys dancing. When the fifers stopped they all crouched down in the street, and when the reed-pipes and the fifes shrilled, and the flat, dry, hollow drums tapped it out again, they all went up in the air dancing. In the crowd you saw only the heads and shoulders of the dancers going up and down.

Did you begin to actually see the crowd in your mind? Did you get a feel for the dancers, the music, and the rockets? Those are the things that can stay with you long after your class is over. More than one person has taken a trip to Pamplona, Spain, to see the festival Hemingway described above.

Another Way In

Sometimes, it's not the action that makes writing interesting. When a story seems to have not much happening, you're going to need to look elsewhere to find the involving part of the book. In cases like these, you're going to need to look at the writing itself. What kind of language does the author use? Are the words ten-syllable monsters you have to look up all the time? Or does it sound like Uncle Otto, sipping his soda while he tells you about driving his pickup off the Talahache bridge? The way the writing sounds is the author's tone, and tone can give you an understanding of the author's attitude and relationship to his characters and their situation.

Read the following passage, paying attention to the tone of the piece. What kind of voice is used? Underline, highlight, and leave notes in the margins about any specific words or phrases that point to the voice and overall tone of the piece.

He was here at Frank Martin's to dry out and to figure how to get his life back on track. But he wasn't here against his will, any more than I was. We weren't locked up. We could leave any time we wanted. But a minimum stay of a week was recommended, and two weeks or a month was, as they put it, "strongly advised."

As I said, this is my second time at Frank Martin's. When I was trying to sign a check to pay in advance for a week's stay, Frank Martin said, "The holidays are always bad. Maybe you should think of sticking around a little longer this time? Think in terms of a couple of weeks. Can you do a couple of weeks? Think about it, anyway. You don't have to decide anything right now," he said. He held his thumb on the check and I signed my name. Then I walked my girlfriend to the front door and said goodbye. "Goodbye," she said, and she lurched into the doorjamb and then onto the porch. It's late afternoon. It's raining. I go from the door to the window. I move the curtain and watch her drive away. She's in my car. She's drunk. But I'm drunk, too, and there's nothing I can do. I make it to a big chair that's close to the radiator, and I sit down. Some guys look up from their TV. Then they shift back to what they were watching. I just sit there. Now and then I look up at something that's happening on the screen.

Later that afternoon the front door banged open and J.P. was brought in between those two big guys—his father-in-law and brother-in-law, I find out afterward. They steered J.P. across the room. The old guy signed him in and gave Frank Martin a check. Then these two guys helped J.P. upstairs. I guess they put him to bed. Pretty soon the old guy and the other guy came downstairs and headed for the front door. They couldn't seem to get out of this place fast enough. It was like they couldn't wait to wash their hands of all this. I didn't blame them. Hell, no. I don't know how I'd act if I was in their shoes.

A day and a half later J.P. and I meet up on the front porch. We shake hands and comment on the weather. J.P. has a case of the shakes. We sit down and prop our feet up on the railing. We lean back in our chairs like we're just out there taking our ease, like we might be getting ready to talk about our bird dogs. That's when J.P. gets going with his story.

These are the type of guys for whom "a couple of weeks" is an unusually long time. They speak in short sentences. They can't even trust long words. These are people living word to word. Do you think these guys will succeed? Is it fact that leads you to this conclusion, or is it the overall tone and attitude of the piece? Is this guy likable? Does he seem like the type to lie? Does this matter? These guys, the narrator and J.P., are struggling against alcoholism at Frank

Martin's, a drying-out place. How people speak and how the author describes things can provide another way for you to get interested in the book and in the characters.

You might remember that I said a few chapters back that it's not worth looking up every word you don't know. Well, that's doubly—no *triply*—true in fiction. Often authors will use a foreign or specific word to say exactly what they mean. They know when they're doing this and will try to make it clear in context why they are using it and just what they mean by it. If they're not using a word in this way, don't worry about it, because it's probably not that important. If they are, don't let that word you don't know slow you down. Put a mark next to it, and plow through to the end of the chapter. If you still haven't figured out the word, then (and only then) look it up. Usually, looking stuff up is counterproductive because it's distracting and time-consuming.

Reading Zone 9

Read the following passage and the answer the questions that follow. You can check your answers on page 245.

> The village of Holcomb stands on the high wheat plains of western Kansas, a lonesome area that other Kansans call "out there." Some seventy miles east of the Colorado border, the countryside, with its hard blue skies and desert-clear air, has an atmosphere that is rather more Far Western than Middle West. The local accent is barbed with a prairie twang, a ranch-hand nasalness, and the men, many of them, wear narrow frontier trousers, Stetsons, and high-heeled boots with pointed toes. The land is flat, and the views are awesomely extensive; horses, herds of cattle, a white cluster of grain elevators rising as gracefully as Greek temples are visible long before a traveler reaches them.

Holcomb, too, can be seen from great distances. Not that there is much to see—simply an aimless congregation of buildings divided in the center by the main-line tracks of the Santa Fe Railroad, a haphazard hamlet bounded on the south by a brown stretch of the Arkansas (pronounced "Ar-kan-sas") River, on the north by a highway, Route 50, and on the east and west by prairie lands and wheat fields. After rain, or when snowfalls thaw, the streets, unnamed, unshaded, unpaved, turn from the thickets dust into the direst mud. At one end of the town stands a stark old stucco structure, the roof of which supports an electric sign—DANCE—but the dancing has ceased and the advertisement has been dark for several years. Nearby is another building with an irrelevant sign, this one is flaking gold on a dirty window—HOLCOMB BANK. The bank closed in 1933, and its former counting rooms have been converted into apartments. It is one of the town's two "apartment houses," the second being a ramshackle mansion known, because a good part of the local school's faculty lives there, as the Teacherage. But the majority of Holcomb's homes are one-story frame affairs, with front porches.

Down by the depot, the postmistress, a gaunt women who wears a rawhide jacket and denims and cowboy boots, presides over a falling-apart post office. The depot itself, with its peeling sulphur-colored paint, is equally melancholy; the Chief, the Super Chief, the El Capitan go by every day, but these celebrated expresses never pause there. No passenger trains do—only an occasional freight. Up on the highway, there are two filling stations, one of which doubles as a meagerly supplied grocery store, while the other does extra duty as a cafe—Hartman's Cafe, where Mrs. Hartman, the proprietress, dispenses sandwiches, coffee, soft drinks, and 3.2 beer. (Holcomb, like all the rest of Kansas, is "dry.")

And that, really, is all. Unless you include, as one must, the Holcomb School, a good-looking establishment, which reveals a circumstance that the appearance of the community otherwise camouflages: that the parent who sent their children to this modern and ably staffed "consolidated" school—the grades go from kindergarten through senior high, and a fleet of buses transport the students, of which there are usually around three hundred and sixty, from as far as sixteen miles away—are, in general, a prosperous people. Farm ranchers, most of them, they are outdoor folk of very varied stock—German, Irish, Norwegian, Mexican, Japanese. They raise cattle and sheep, grow wheat, milo grass seed, and sugar beets. Farming is always a chancey business, but in western Kansas its practitioners consider themselves "born gamblers," for they must contend with an extremely shallow precipitation (the annual average is eighteen inches) and anguishing irrigation problems. However, the last seven years have been years of drought-less beneficence. The farm ranchers in Finney County, of which Holcomb is a part, have done well; money has been made not from farming alone but also from the exploita-tion of plentiful natural-gas resources, and its acquisition is reflected in the new school, the comfortable interiors of the farmhouses, the steep and swollen grain elevators.

Until one morning in mid-November of 1959, few Americans—in fact, few Kansans—had ever heard of Hol-comb. Like the waters of the river, like the motorists on the highway, and like the yellow trains streaking down the Santa Fe track, drama, in the shape of exceptional hap-penings, had never stopped there. The inhabitants of the village, numbering two hundred and seventy, were satisfied that this should be so, quite content to exist inside ordinary life—to work, to hunt, to watch television, to attend school socials, choir practice, meetings of the 4-H Club. But then, in the earliest hours of that morning in November, a cer-tain Sunday morning, certain foreign sounds impinged on the normal nightly Holcomb noises—on the keening hyste-ria of coyotes, the dry scrape of scuttling tumbleweed, the racing, receding wail of locomotive whistles. At the time not a soul in sleeping Holcomb heard them—four shotgun blasts that, all told, ended six human lives. But afterward the townspeople, theretofore sufficiently unfearful of each other to seldom trouble to lock their doors, found fantasy re-creating them over and again—those somber explo-sions that stimulated fires of mistrust in the glare of which many old neighbors viewed each other strangely, and as strangers.

1. According to the passage, the word "hamlet" could best be defined as
   (A) an urban center
   (B) a Prince of Denmark
   (C) a train station
   (D) a small town
   (E) a river-bounded island

2. The tone of the passage can best be described as primarily
   (A) journalistic
   (B) explosive
   (C) technical
   (D) tragic
   (E) personal

3. The best description of Holcomb before the shotgun blasts would be
   (A) homogeneous and peaceful
   (B) volatile and isolationist
   (C) frightened and unfriendly
   (D) placid and picturesque
   (E) impoverished and picaresque

4. The violence of the shotgun blasts seemed, to the author, to be
   (A) an expected occurrence, predictable in this violent town
   (B) a rare occurrence in an otherwise regularly violent town
   (C) a shocking occurrence, forever changing this otherwise peaceful town
   (D) a welcome occurrence, breaking the monotony of the otherwise boring town
   (E) a painful occurrence, embraced and forgiven by this otherwise picturesque town

5. It can be inferred from the passage that the people killed by the shotgun blasts were
   (A) strangers visiting the town
   (B) relatives of a member of the town
   (C) criminals who lived near the town
   (D) residents of the town
   (E) the founders of Holcomb, Kansas

Reflection

For any question you got wrong, go back and leave notes next to each answer choice indicating why it is correct or incorrect. It's important that you not only practice, but also reflect on your performance! This way, you'll see what issues give you trouble and gain a better understanding of how to improve.

Chapter 9 Summary

- Reading a novel or book of short stories requires more commitment than does reading a newspaper article or chapter in a textbook, for example. Don't expect to finish a novel in a day.

- Set realistic goals for yourself. Dedicate thirty or as little as fifteen minutes a day to reading.

- If you're reading for an assignment, use strategies to keep yourself engaged in the text. Learning about the author, for instance, can increase your interest in a work of literature and give it more meaning.

- Pay attention to the title of the work or any quotes that appear at the beginning of the novel (or any other work of fiction). These can often point to the theme of the work.

- Theme-marking will help you keep track of a certain image or character, in turn allowing you to make connections and clarify the meaning of the text.

- Read a work of fiction like you would watch a movie. Visualize what's going on in your mind and use images to help bring the story to life.

- Focus on literary devices like language, word choice, tone, voice, and point of view. All of these devices can help you understand the greater meaning of a work.

Fiction: Part 2

"That's what fiction is for. It's for getting at the truth when the truth isn't sufficient for the truth."

—Tim O'Brien

Fiction on Your Own

In the previous chapter, we discussed how to read fiction for school and assignments—all work, no play. This chapter, though, turns to reading fiction for leisure. Now that you don't have to theme-mark, and you don't have to keep track of every single fact, you are somewhat liberated. Doesn't it feel good? It's like the difference between playing an organized game of basketball and just shooting some baskets. Enjoy the process—you don't need to remember everything, and no one is going to yell at you if you don't do everything perfectly.

Don't use this as an excuse to read without a plan, or to keep the television on in the background. If you do that, you're just going to read the same way as before, too slowly and without enough involvement. Use this chance to throw yourself only into the parts that really interest you. Pay attention to the things you like. This will allow you to read more actively.

How do you know that you're going to want to put some effort into a book? Well, read the first chapter. The author generally uses the first chapter to set up the plot, the characters, and the themes that continue throughout the novel. If the first chapter doesn't grab you, then it is unlikely the rest of the novel will. Some books do take a while to get going—but usually they don't have terrible first chapters, only mildly unpleasant ones. Many novels don't live up to the promise of their first chapters, but you can certainly eliminate the novels which you immediately hate, don't understand, or are in a language you don't know.

Divide and Conquer

Most modern popular fiction divides itself into sections within chapters. Often, each section will take care of some requirement of the author, whether it's plot development, character development, or description. You can quickly tell by reading the first few sentences of a section what the focus of the section is going to be. If only one of these three interests you, you can skip the other two types of sections. Of course, you're going to miss a whole bunch of the book, but if you can still piece together the story, who cares? It's not like a dinner where you have to eat your vegetables to get your dessert. If you want to skip to the last chapter of a murder mystery, go ahead. The literature police won't come after you. There are no rules—you get out of a book what you put in.

Exercise 10

See if you can quickly tell what each of these sections is going to focus on: plot, character, or setting. Use the line below each paragraph to note what type of section you think it is. You can check your answers on page 246.

1. Paul set the timer on the explosive for two minutes. Barely enough time to get out of the warehouse. If the guards were asleep, and if the silent alarms had not been tripped, he would have a chance. A slim chance.

   _____

2. Carl's hair was like liquid fire. His nails, manicured crescent moons of delight. As his fingers danced along the piano keys, one was reminded of dolphins jumping from the water in the sparkling Aegean.

   _____

3. In the past, his brother had helped him out of jams like this. Before that, it was his father. And as a little kid, it had been his mother. People were always taking care of Johnny. But here, alone in a strange town, with no one who knew his face, his name, he started helping others, and, one morning, as he was jump-starting a car stuck in a snowbank, he realized that he had become his own person.

   _____

4. Mathilda thought that kissing John had been fun, but pointless. He was always making these silly noises, and she was always afraid her older sister would see her smeared lipstick. She would rather ride the carnival rides, feel the whooping feel of the up-and-down roller coaster, the arms of the octopus, the drop of the free-fall machine.

_____

5. Uncle Walvis stumbled through the streets of Newark, raising the sleeping residents with his bagpipe music. He lurched from side to side, warbling out his unsteady tunes, as a strange thing, almost like a vision, began to take place. Walvis noticed people watching from the windows, staring in disbelief and pointing at him as he played. Uncertain, confused, he turned around: He was followed by an army of wombats, wombats of all sizes, entranced by the uneven grating of Walvis' pipes.

_____

6. Charles browsed through the library looking for a book on Mary Queen of Scots, or, if they didn't have one, a book on the lottery. He didn't care. He liked the feel of shelves, filled with books, of dusty, unused leather, and of enforced silence. Often, in his room, late at night, he would imagine he was in the library and force himself to be silent, and if he was bad, he would fine himself fifty cents.

_____

7. Brenda slapped Dillon with a paternity suit. He was shocked. Sure, he had a gambling problem. And contract negotiations for next year weren't going well. But everyone knew that being slapped with a paternity suit would mean the end of his career. He wished, prayed, that he was related to the producer of his show, and that he could be talentless but be guaranteed a job.

_____

8. Vicki didn't just hate Carol—she despised her. Everything Carol did was great, and universally loved, even that stupid ear pull she closed every show with. And everything Vicki did was a copy, a rip-off, a no-talent solution. She would show them all. She planned in her sleep all the secrets she would tell to the tabloids. When she was done, Carol would wish she had never trifled with a redhead like Vicki!

---

9. The sun fell like light rain on the copper roof, sparkling with golden glares and sharp points. It was difficult to look at—it hurt the eyes. But everything else looked dull, unwashed next to that roof. The porch looked cracked and rotting, the railing looked warm-eaten and dying. The brown patch of dirt which was called the lawn lifted small dust-devils of turf smoke across the base of the stairs and up to the crack underneath the flapping screen door.

The Short Story

If you think that reading a short story will take you less time than a novel, you're right. Short stories are shorter. Even so, you should put just as much thought into the act of reading a short story as you would a longer piece of fiction. A short story can be just as complicated, as dense, and as powerful as any novel. Because it is a distilled form of fiction, every image and symbol becomes correspondingly more important and significant. If you don't believe me, try reading any Flannery O'Connor or Charlotte Perkins Gilman story. Theme-marking, summarizing, and figuring out one of those stories can take a *long* time. And hopefully, the story will be exciting and interesting to you because the hidden elements all add to the dynamic, creative storytelling.

Some people really dislike short stories; they see them as unsatisfying, incomplete, and confusing. Some people also hate chocolate—there's no accounting for taste. Be open-minded when it comes to short stories. Take each story on its own merits. You're going to like some more than others. It's just important that you give them a chance.

Reading Zone 10

Read the following passage as if you were reading it just for leisure. Do not time yourself; the point of this exercise is to see how much of the passage you retain. Then answer the questions that follow and check your answers on page 246.

> Sheppard sat on a stool at the bar that divided the kitchen in half, eating his cereal out of the individual pasteboard box it came in. He ate mechanically, his eyes on the child, who was wandering from cabinet to cabinet in the paneled kitchen, collecting the ingredients for his breakfast. He was a stocky blond boy of ten. Sheppard kept his intense blue eyes fixed on him. The boy's future was written in his face. He would be a banker. No, worse. He would operate a small loan company. All he wanted for the child was

that he be good and unselfish and neither seemed likely. Sheppard was a young man whose hair was already white. It stood up like a narrow brush halo over his pink sensitive face.

The boy approached the bar with a jar of peanut butter under his arm, a plate with a quarter of a small chocolate cake on it in one hand and the ketchup bottle in the other. He did not appear to notice his father. He climbed up on the stool and began to spread peanut butter on the cake. He had very round large ears that leaned away from his head and seemed to pull his eyes slightly too far apart. His shirt was green but so faded that the cowboy across the front of it was only a shadow.

"Norton," Sheppard said, "I saw Rufus Johnson yesterday. Do you know what he was doing?"

The child looked at him with a kind of half attention, his eyes half forward but not yet engaged. They were a paler blue than his father's as if they might have faded like the shirt; one of them listed, almost imperceptibly, toward the outer rim.

"He was in an alley," Sheppard said, "and he had his hand in a garbage can. He was trying to get something to eat out of it." He paused to let this soak in. "He was hungry," he finished, and tried to pierce the child's conscience with his gaze.

The boy picked up the piece of chocolate cake and began to gnaw it from one corner. "Norton," Sheppard said, "do you have any idea of what it means to share?" A flicker of attention. "Some of it's yours," Norton said. "Some of it's his," Sheppard said heavily. It was hopeless. Almost any fault would have been preferable to selfishness—a violent temper, even a tendency to lie.

The child turned the bottle of ketchup upside-down and began thumping ketchup onto the cake. Sheppard's look of pain increased. "You are ten and Rufus Johnson is fourteen," he said. "Yet I'm sure your shirts would fit Rufus." Rufus Johnson was a boy he had been trying to help at the reformatory for the past year. He had been released two months ago. "When he was in the reformatory, he looked pretty good, but when I saw him yesterday, he was skin and bones. He hadn't been eating cake with peanut butter on it for breakfast."

"It's stale," he said. "That's why I have to put stuff on it."

Sheppard turned his face to the window at the end of the bar. The side lawn, green and even, sloped fifty feet or so down to a small suburban wood. When his wife was living, they had often eaten outside, even breakfast, on the grass. He had never noticed then that the child was selfish. "Listen to me," he said, turning back to him, "look at me and listen." The boy looked at him. At least his eyes were forward. "I gave Rufus a key to this house when he left the reformatory—to show my confidence in him and so he would have a place he could come to and feel welcome any time. He didn't use it, but I think he'll use it now because he's seen me and he's hungry. And if he doesn't use it I'm going out and find him and bring him here. I can't see a child eating out of garbage cans." The boy frowned. It was dawning on him that something of his was threatened. Sheppard's mouth stretched in disgust. "Rufus's father died before he was born," he said. "His mother is in the state penitentiary. He was raised by his grandfather in a shack without water or electricity and the old man beat him every day. How would you like to belong to a family like that?" "I don't know," the child said lamely. "Well, you might think about it sometime," Sheppard said.

Sheppard was City Recreational Director. On Saturdays he worked at the reformatory as a counselor, receiving nothing for it but the satisfaction of knowing he was helping boys no one else cared about. Johnson was the most intelligent boy he had worked with and the most deprived. Norton turned the rest of the cake over as if he no longer wanted it. "You started that, now finish it," Sheppard said. "Maybe he won't come," the child said and his eyes brightened slightly. "Think of everything you have that he doesn't!" Sheppard said. "Suppose you had to root in garbage cans for food? Suppose you had a huge swollen foot and one side of you dropped lower than the other when you walked?" The boy looked blank, obviously unable to imagine such a thing. "You have a healthy body," Sheppard said, "a good home. You've never been taught anything but the truth. Your daddy gives you anything you need or want. You don't have a grandfather who beats you. And your mother is not in the state penitentiary." The child pushed his plate away. Sheppard groaned aloud.

A knot of flesh appeared below the boy's suddenly distorted mouth. His face became a mass of lumps with slits for eyes. "If she was in the penitentiary," he began in a kind of racking bellow, "I could go to seeeeee her." Tears rolled down his face and the ketchup dribbled on his chin. He looked as if he had been hit in the mouth. He abandoned himself and howled. Sheppard sat helpless and miserable, like a man lashed by some elemental force of nature. This was not a normal grief. It was all part of his selfishness. She had been dead for over a year and a child's grief should not last so long. "You're going on eleven years old," he said reproachfully. The child began an agonizing high-pitched heaving noise. "If you stop thinking about yourself and think what you can do for somebody else," Sheppard said, "then you'll stop missing your mother." The boy was silent but his shoulders continued to shake. Then his face collapsed and he began to howl again. "Don't you think I'm lonely without her too?" Sheppard said. "Don't you think I miss her at all? I do, but I'm not sitting around moping. I'm busy helping other people. When do you see me just sitting around thinking about my troubles?" The boy slumped as if he were exhausted but fresh tears streaked his face.

"What are you going to do today?" Sheppard asked, to get his mind on something else. The child ran his arm across his eyes. "Sell seeds," he mumbled. Always selling something. He had four quart jars full of nickels and dimes he had saved and he took them out of his closet every few days and counted them. "What are you selling seeds for?"

"To win a prize."

"What's the prize?"

"A thousand dollars."

"And what would you do if you had a thousand dollars?"

"Keep it," the child said and wiped his nose on his shoulder.

"I feel sure you would," Sheppard said. "Listen," he said and lowered his voice to an almost pleading tone, "suppose by some chance you did win a thousand dollars. Wouldn't you like to spend it on children less fortunate than yourself? Wouldn't you like to give some swings and trapezes to the orphanage? Wouldn't you like to buy poor Rufus Johnson a new shoe?"

The boy began to back away from the bar. Then suddenly he leaped forward and hung with his mouth open over his plate. Sheppard groaned again. Everything came up, the cake, the peanut butter, the ketchup—a limp sweet batter. He hung over it gagging, more came, and he waited with his mouth open over the plate as if he expected his heart to come up next.

1. The relationship between Norton and Sheppard can best be described as
   - (A) loving and open
   - (B) aggressive and violent
   - (C) uncommunicative and disjointed
   - (D) sickening and unnatural
   - (E) friendly and supportive

2. According to Sheppard, operating a small loan company would be
   - (A) a sign of self-involvement
   - (B) a lucrative career move
   - (C) a fate similar to losing one's soul
   - (D) an unlikelihood for Norton
   - (E) a good job for Norton

3. How does the author intend the reader to interpret Sheppard's name?
   - (A) Ironically
   - (B) Symbolically
   - (C) Humorously
   - (D) Incorrectly
   - (E) No interpretation

4. Why does the author keep referring to the character as "the child" instead of "Norton"?
   (A) To make the reader dislike him
   (B) Because Sheppard dislikes him
   (C) To establish distance between the two characters
   (D) To establish distance between Norton and the reader
   (E) To distinguish between Rufus and Norton

5. According to Sheppard, what's the least desirable fault someone can have?
   (A) A violent temper
   (B) Selfishness
   (C) A tendency to lie
   (D) Putting ketchup on cake
   (E) Operating a loan company

Reflection

For any question you got wrong, go back and leave notes next to each answer choice indicating why it is correct or incorrect. It's important that you not only practice, but also reflect on your performance! This way, you'll see what issues give you trouble and gain a better understanding of how to improve.

Chapter 10 Summary

- If you're unsure whether you want to put the effort into reading a novel or other work of fiction, read the first chapter. This will give you a sense of the writing style, characters, and plot, and thus allow you to gauge how well the book will hold your interest.

- When reading for leisure, you don't have to worry about remembering every detail about the plot or characters. However, pay attention to the parts that interest you. Doing so will allow you to read more actively and be just as engaged as you would be when reading for an assignment or test.

- Though shorter than novels, short stories are dense with symbols and images that take time to unravel and figure out. Therefore, you need to put just as much effort into reading a short story as you would a longer work of fiction.

CHAPTER 11

Journalism

"If I want to knock a story off the front page, I just change my hairstyle."

—Hillary Rodham Clinton

Journalism as Literature

Before you start this chapter, grab a newspaper or a magazine—try to find one without a lot of perfume ads, unless you want a headache. When you get a chance, go to the magazine area of your local bookstore or medical waiting office. Look at the huge number of magazines and newspapers that each cater to a specific audience: *Glamour, Vogue, The New York Times, Wall Street Journal, Mad Magazine, Brides Magazine, U.S. News and World Report*. It seems that if you are interested in anything, there is a magazine for you (or there will be one shortly). And most of the time, when you pick up a magazine to read, you're not exactly sure what you're going to need it for. An article may seem interesting for the first few paragraphs, but often people just put down the magazine or newspaper, bored, confused, or annoyed, because the article didn't turn out to be about what they expected to read.

Journalism is one of the most diverse fields of literature, in both style and content. You have to be prepared for anything, from a dull, sleep-inducing recitation of events to a vibrant, argumentative piece on a volatile issue based mainly on opinion. Once you learn to quickly identify what kind of piece you're looking at, you're in good shape with this type of reading. The first thing you must keep in mind is that for any piece of journalism, the author is arguing a point. Oh, sure, the *Wall Street Journal* may sound less opinionated than *Revolution Today*, but if you look closely, the former is arguing its point just as fiercely—if more subtly.

The second thing you have to look for is the difference between opinion and fact. Often, it's the journalist's job to use certain facts to get you to feel a certain way. (This may seem like a cynical point of view, but just look at many pieces published during election cycles). By distinguishing fact from opinion, you can tell what the true situation is versus what the author wants you to feel. Sometimes the author is wrong—and by figuring out what the facts are, you can start to argue with the article's conclusions. Let's look at an example of a journalistic piece that appears just to be *stating* the facts, but in reality *argues* a point. Make an effort to distinguish fact from opinion.

Legend has it that Thomas Edison was a champion napper. A couple of times every day, he would sit peacefully in a chair with a solid iron ball in each hand. As he moved from light sleeping to deep slumber, the balls would drop and wake him up, thus preventing him from falling into a deep sleep.

Edison knew what he was doing. Says Dr. Claudio Stampi, a sleeping disorders expert at the Institute for Circadian Physiology in Cambridge, Massachusetts: "The most restful nap with the least amount of sleep-hangover is between 15 and 30 minutes." Many historical figures have enhanced their productive powers, and probably increased their life spans, by napping. Among them: Leonardo da Vinci, Winston Churchill, Albert Einstein, John F. Kennedy, Ronald Reagan, and basketball's Wilt Chamberlain. Yet when asked, nearly half of all adult Americans stoutly deny that they ever nap. Stampi, who is one of the few scientists to focus on the subject of napping, thinks most people equate the practice with indolence or old age.

Stampi is bent on making napping respectable. Some intriguing new research supports his cause. Historically, American society had been geared to what biologists call a "monophasic" sleep/awake pattern, in which the day is rigidly divided into one period of wakefulness, followed by one period of sleep. Under the monophasic model, napping has been considered culturally inappropriate and, according to some experts in the field of sleep research, even unhealthy, in that it cuts into night-time sleeping. But new data suggest that human beings may in fact be "biphasic" creatures whose days are broken up into two periods of sleep, nocturnal and midafternoon. Lunch is commonly blamed as the cause of midafternoon drowsiness, but it turns out that food intake has little or nothing to do with the urge to nod off. Much more important, according to recent research at the Circadian Institute and the University of Pennsylvania, is simply the time of day.

Circadian's Claudio Stampi is convinced that Americans will be better rested, healthier, and more productive if they give in to that urge to take a siesta. Like many sleep disorder researchers, he believes that Americans' "sleep deficit" has steadily grown as people experience more stress in managing the competing needs of careers and families. Far from being a sign of laziness, napping, he says, is really a biological imperative that allows people to whittle away at the deficit.

After you read this article, did you start thinking, "Maybe I should start napping?" (We did.) But once you look closely at the writing, you can see how the author manipulates us into reaching that conclusion. Let's take a look at how the article does this.

Now, what is the author arguing? You can breeze quickly through the facts of the opening paragraphs. It's interesting that Edison, Kennedy, and da Vinci all napped, but did napping make them geniuses? Many people we know nap, and they have yet to discover a basic scientific principle, give moral guidance to a nation, or paint a single chapel ceiling. (This principle is an example of the difference between primary and secondary facts, which we explained in Chapter 7.) The author is presenting a little snapshot of Claudio Stampi and, in so doing, arguing his point that people should nap. How does the author do this without saying straight out she believes Stampi?

In a few ways. First, she cites historical figures meant to inspire us who support Stampi's point of view. This is meant to ally us with Stampi's opinion (implied: Do you want to be like Albert Einstein? Then nap!) Second, when she describes Stampi's research she uses the adjective "intriguing." Intriguing means "thought-provoking," which she tries to do, to change the way we think about sleep. She cites only Stampi's new research, and doesn't present any opposing point of view. And finally, she ends up agreeing with Stampi's conclusion. If her conclusion is Stampi's conclusion, then our conclusion should be Stampi's conclusion. This piece masterfully manipulates the reader by choosing selective facts and presenting them in a certain way. Should we be mad at the author for doing this to us in her piece? Absolutely not. It's her job to get us to feel a certain way about facts. Heck, if we feel anything, she's done a good job. The author has here argued successfully for us to change our thoughts. We should be impressed by her good work.

Therefore, be a skeptical reader. Don't take opinion or selective fact as the final truth. If someone told you that seventy five percent of Americans are in favor of burning witches, would you believe him? How about twenty five percent? Big manipulations of fact (lies, that is) are easy to spot. To spot the small manipulations of numbers or facts which subtly support the author's point, you have to be vigilant. By uncovering the author's argument, you can start to look at the facts and see how objective they are.

What if the question were asked in the following way: "If we could prove that certain people, without any doubt, were witches, and had ceased to be human hundreds of years ago, that they were planning an overthrow of the world which would succeed and lead to pain and misery for all human-kind, and the only way to stop them (regrettably) would be to immolate them, in that case, would you object to our saving your way of life?" You might expect a majority response of "No, I don't mind. Immolate 'em." Also, people might not realize that "immolate" means "setting on fire." But the following question might get a different response: "If I think someone's a witch, I should burn them, right?" Most people would be less likely to agree with the second question. But both percentages could be used as facts in an article to support a point of view. You should be suspicious of articles that claim to present only the truth, particularly ones that appear to have no point of view. Those are the most dangerous of all—their authors are working behind the scenes to get you to feel one way or another. The best defense against being manipulated by an article is to quickly identify the author's argument.

How do you figure out an author's argument? Ask yourself some questions about the article. First of all, where is it from? Usually, a magazine or a newspaper will have a tradition of a certain point of view. For example, the *Utne Reader* contains alternative, non-traditional approaches to contemporary issues. So if an article in the *Utne Reader* is titled "Cars and America," you can probably expect something that challenges a traditional notion of the relationship between cars and America. The same article in *Car and Driver* will have completely different content and a completely different point of view. Where you are reading is important—don't forget about it.

Begin at the Beginning

The second thing that you want to know is the title of the article. Many articles will have a heading and then a subheading. You can use these things to identify what the article is going to be about. For example, several articles can be titled "The Year 2020" but have different subheadings which quickly identify which one is more important to you.

"The Year 2020: Global Crisis or World Peace?"

"The Year 2020: Stocks to Buy for the Future"

"The Year 2020: An Adventure in Cooking"

"The Year 2020: Colonizing Mars"

"The Year 2020: Your Horoscope for the Future"

"The Year 2020: Cancer is Now History"

"The Year 2020: Dating Tips for Robots"

All of these are written for different groups, and one is not necessarily more important than another. It depends on what is most important in your life and what you are interested in. Use all the available information to tell you what is the right article for you. Headlines, kickers, and headers are useful ways to scan quickly which articles will be of interest to you.

Find Out When

When was it written? You might think this isn't important, but it helps you figure out some of the author's direction. The title of an article from the *Bethlehem Gazette* reads "How Smoking Matures You" and the article goes on to support smoking as a healthy, pleasant endeavor. This article was written in 1911. An article from 1986 on the stock market might have been titled "Why The Market Will Never Fall." In 1987, the stock market lost 22.8% of its value in one day, falling over 508 points. With the knowledge you have now, you judge these articles differently. The date of publication affects how current, useful, and trustworthy the information is.

These ideas aren't new. You know about identifying what you read from Chapter 1. We're just asking you to make it to a different level now. The more you know about what you're reading, the more you'll retain. Of course, as we've stressed before, why you're reading is as important as what you're reading, and it should affect your approach to the material. If you're reading for pleasure, take what you like from the material (as long as you take enough to follow the author's argument). If you're reading for retention or to bolster your knowledge on a certain topic, sort out the irrelevant or less relevant facts from what you really need, keeping only the good stuff.

Are You Hortense or Eunice?

Hortense and Eunice are both at the zoo. Hortense has to write a paper for school on the Stinky Crested Wallabee, but Eunice is there for fun. It would be silly for Hortense to wander through every exhibit, memorizing the feeding periods of the Flaming Pit Viper or the number of eggs laid by the Flemish Hooting Walloon, until she gets to the Wallabee cage, just as it would be silly to pay great attention to the Thomas Edison bit in the previous article if what you really need is to research REM sleep. Conversely, Eunice is at the zoo for fun, and she doesn't have to see any pit vipers at all if she doesn't want to. If you're reading for fun, your idea of fun involves primarily stories about Thomas Edison, then that's the only part you have to read.

Reading Zone 11

Read the following passage and answer the questions that follow. You can check your answers on page 247.

The demise of the Soviet Union has, paradoxically, given Vietnam a strategic usefulness to the United States that it never had during a war in which fifty-eight thousand Americans perished. The Soviet collapse has created a power vacuum in East Asia. The American withdrawal from the Philippines and the shrinking of the United States military because of the end of the Cold War and economic troubles at home are contributing to the sense of a power vacuum. This may be more perception than reality, since the United States retains the air and naval capability to assert itself in East Asia, but perception has a reality of its own. The Chinese perceive it, and they are intent on filling the vacuum.

Southern China is an economic astonishment. Guangdong Province's economy, for example, grew at an average annual rate of fifteen per cent from 1981 to 1991. The Chinese are using their new wealth to make themselves the big military power in the region. They are creating a sophisticated Air Force, purchasing long-range Sukhoi-27 fighter-bombers, MIG-31 interceptors, and airborne surveillance- and-control planes from Russia. They are bringing their Army up to date with Russia's latest T-72 main battle tanks. Beijing is also building a "blue water" Navy to project force beyond China's shores, negotiating with Russia and Ukraine for an aircraft carrier that was under construction at a Soviet shipyard.

Like it or not, the United States is going to have to play the role of regional balancer—the guarantor of stability in the last resort—to keep China from unsettling East Asia in the post-Cold War era. There is too much to lose for us to refuse the role. Americans tend to view their current relationship with Asia as a one-way drain of cash to Japan. The street has lanes that go in both directions. American two-way trade with Asia and the Pacific exceeded $360 billion in 1992, and roughly 2.6 million jobs in the United

States are dependent on it. United States exports more to Singapore than it does to Spain or Italy, and American firms have about $66 billion invested in that part of the world.

Lifting the economic embargo, opening diplomatic relations, and backing the cause of economic reform in Vietnam to strengthen the country by quickening its development would serve the American need to counter Chinese regional ambitions. The relationship suits the Vietnamese, because big nations that do not threaten their independence, as the United States no longer does, are the kinds of friends the Vietnamese want. The Vietnamese assume, rightly or wrongly, that the more involved American business is in Vietnam, the more China will hesitate to move against them. Tom Vallely, a Harvard Vietnam specialist, who first went to the country as a nineteen-year-old Marine infantryman and is now trying to help the Vietnamese shift to a market economy, quipped "One Mobil oil rig in the South China Sea is worth the whole Seventh Fleet."

The looming threat of China propels the Vietnamese attempt to make peace with the United States. When Deng Xiaoping invaded Vietnam in 1979, after the Vietnamese drove China's Cambodian protégé, the homicidal Khmer Rouge, out of Phnom Penh, Vietnamese troops were able to halt the Chinese rapidly and bloody them badly, because they were in excellent fighting trim. Yet the ultimate checkrein on Chinese behavior that has since vanished was the threat of Soviet retaliation. The Vietnamese also relied on the Soviet Union for their weaponry. With their benefactors now history, Vietnamese armament has become outmoded.

While Vietnam has made peace with China and full trade and diplomatic relations have resumed, the Chinese seem to want more: they seem to want submission. The visit to Vietnam last December of Li Peng, the Chinese premier, went badly. Peng behaved as if he were visiting a tributary. China has so far been the winner in Cambodia, because its cat's-paw, the Khmer Rouge, has succeeded in sabotaging the United Nations peace plan and once again constitutes a menace to the Vietnamese.

1. Which of the following excerpts is not an opinion?
   (A) "[A] checkrein on Chinese behavior that has since vanished was the threat of the Soviet Union."
   (B) "Like it or not, the United States is going to have to play the role of regional balancer...to keep China from unsettling East Asia in the post-Cold War era. There is too much to lose for us to refuse the role."
   (C) "Lifting the economic embargo, opening diplomatic relations, and backing the cause of economic reform in Vietnam to strengthen the country by quickening its development would serve the American need to counter Chinese regional ambitions."
   (D) "One Mobil oil rig in the South China Sea is worth the whole Seventh Fleet."
   (E) "The looming threat of China propels the Vietnamese attempt to make peace with the United States."

2. Which of the following quotations is a primary fact?
   (A) "Guangdong Province's economy...grew at an average annual rate of fifteen percent from 1981 to 1991."
   (B) "American two-way trade with Asia and the Pacific exceeded $360 billion in 1992, and roughly 2.6 million jobs in the United States are dependent on it."
   (C) "When Deng Xiaoping invaded Vietnam in 1979... Vietnamese troops were able to halt the Chinese rapidly and bloody them badly."
   (D) "The Chinese are using their new wealth to make themselves a big military power in the region."
   (E) "[The Chinese] are purchasing long-range Sukhoi-27 fighter-bombers, MIG-31 interceptors, and airborne surveillance-and-control planes from Russia."

3. Which sentence best summarizes the author's argument?
   (A) The Chinese may attack Vietnam again.
   (B) The United States views Vietnam as a bulwark against Chinese aggression.
   (C) Both Vietnam and the United States would benefit from a normalization of relations.
   (D) Vietnam fears Chinese domination.
   (E) The dissolution of the Soviet Union has fundamentally changed the United States-Vietnam relationship.

4. According to the passage, all of the following contributes to the perceived power vacuum in East Asia EXCEPT
   (A) the American withdrawal from the Philippines
   (B) the shrinking U.S. military budget
   (C) the Vietnamese disarmament along Cambodian borders
   (D) the collapse of the Soviet Union
   (E) American domestic economic struggles

5. According to the author, which of the following is the primary reason behind Vietnam's attempt to make peace with the United States?
   (A) Investment opportunities in U.S. oil companies
   (B) The looming threat of China
   (C) Li Peng's ill-fated visit
   (D) The threat of the Khmer Rouge
   (E) China's annual economic growth rate

6. America's financial relationship with the East is
   (A) often misconstrued
   (B) dependent in both directions
   (C) valued at approximately 66 billion dollars
   (D) all of the above
   (E) none of the above

7. According to the passage, in the face of global demilitarization, China is
   (A) seeking most-favored nation trading status
   (B) ignoring human rights violations
   (C) aggressively pushing into Cambodia
   (D) rearming with modern weaponry
   (E) pursuing economic growth aggressively

8. The author's main reason for why the United States must "play the role of regional balancer" is inherently
   (A) economic
   (B) moral
   (C) political
   (D) military
   (E) social

9. We can infer from the passage that since 1979 Vietnam's relationship with China has been
   (A) improving
   (B) degenerating
   (C) satisfactory to China
   (D) satisfactory to Vietnam
   (E) satisfactory to both

10. What, according to the passage, would the United States gain from an open relationship with Vietnam?
    (A) A downsizing of the United States military presence
    (B) The capability to assert itself financially in Eastern Europe
    (C) A Vietnamese shift to market economy
    (D) A military presence in the Far East
    (E) Oil resources

I Saw the Sign

Much in the way that highway signs tell you where a road leads, what towns are accessible from each exit, and what other roads are available, headers and quotations pulled out from an article ("kickers," they are called) tell you what to expect from different parts of an article. Remember pre-reading? Scan the article quickly for headers and kickers that tell you about the way the facts are broken up. Use them to guide your reading through any article. Do you need certain information about the history of a neighborhood? Do you need the facts in a murder case? Are you just looking for the scores in a sporting event? The headers and kickers will tell you where to look.

For example, in a *Business Week* cover story article on former President Bill Clinton's second year in office, the following headers subdivided the article into these parts:

- Policy Grafts
- Shooting Sprees
- Health Security
- Pension Security
- Education and Training
- Competitiveness Policy
- Personal Safety
- "No Testosterone"

Each of these can point you to a section of the article that would provide details and opinions on that facet of Clinton's second year. By using the headers, you can quickly jump to the portion of the article you need to read without having to read all the other stuff. Each section contains one discrete subject (and even an indiscreet one—if you don't get the joke, look up the definitions of *discrete* and *discreet* right now). This brings us to an important point. Do you want to read everything in every article in every paper and every magazine? Noooo. You want to choose the articles that are important to you, so scan the headlines, headers, photographs, and quotes that go with each article. If it is even tangentially related to a topic that is important to you, pre-read the whole thing. If it isn't, move on to the next article. In this way, you've made sure you've covered all your bases. What if you don't know? Read it anyway. It's better to err on the side of being over-informed than under-informed. That's not to suggest that you should read every part of every article: over-informed and out of time is no improvement at all. You've got to read smart—use your judgment on what's important in any given article.

Read Less, Know More

Even when you want to read an article, do you want to read every word or phrase? Again, absolutely not. Why waste time? Skim and increase your speed. But when you read an article or opinion-ated piece, only read as far into any paragraph until you get the main idea of that paragraph. Do not read any further. This sounds strange, but it really works. For a dramatic example, let's look at the first sentence—and only the first sentence—of each paragraph of an old newspaper article on former President Bill Clinton's proposed budget:

Paragraph 1: *Senate Minority Leader Bob Dole said yesterday that he anticipated there would be some Republican support for the budget President Bill Clinton unveiled today. Clinton will need all the support he can get for this budget.*

Paragraph 2: *Rep. Kwesi Mfume (D-Md.) said yesterday he "was not satisfied."*

Paragraph 3: *Clinton will propose cutting mass transit operating subsidies, low-income heating assistance, and new construction money for low-income public housing.*

Paragraph 4: *White House budget director Leon Panetta defended the budget.*

Paragraph 5: *Panetta said the Federal Government will continue to fund mass transit capital spending.*

Paragraph 6: *Panetta said the budget will include healthy increases for technology, training, and education.*

Paragraph 7: *Dole, meanwhile, noted the president's budget was in some ways incomplete.*

Purists and news junkies are probably tearing their hair after reading the above "news," but face it, our condensed version is about as informative as most TV news programs, and reading it took far less time than either watching TV news or reading the entire article would have taken. Now you have the time to get into loud blustering arguments about issues of unimaginable complexity, like the budget, based on just a few sentences you lifted out of context.

Exercise 11.1

Here's an exercise that you'll have to grade yourself on. Grab that newspaper you've had sitting by you since you started this chapter, and find a dull article about something important. The business section is a good place to start. Now read only the first sentence of each paragraph (if you can't help peeking, use an index card to block the rest of the paragraph). Using your newfound powers of retention, write down every important fact you can remember: names, dates, amounts, and, of course, the subject of the article. Now go back and read the whole article, and make a similar list. If you compare the two, you'll find that your lists are similar in length, meaning that you absorbed about the same amount of information from each reading. Your second list may be a little longer, but look at the items that appear only on the second list. Are they primary or secondary facts? Do they really add to your basic understanding of the topic? No, because if they did, they'd have their own paragraph with their own introductory sentence.

Repeat this exercise with a couple of different articles. Try a sports article. Try a fashion article. Try topics you wouldn't normally read about. Not only will you be learning about reading more efficiently, you'll also become a more well-rounded human being.

Mapping the Argument

Argument mapping means laying out all the points an author makes in the order she makes them. This process exposes the structure of the argument, and therefore, its weaknesses. You'd want your surgeon to know anatomy, wouldn't you? Maybe a little chemistry? Knowledge of structure tells you the author's position, point of view, the facts of the argument, and the flaws. Without seeing the structure, some of these flaws can slip by you.

See the Structure

You'll notice that when you look at the beginning of each paragraph, the first sentences form an outline of the story. That's intentional. Given their strict space requirements, reporters have to get their information across in as direct a manner as possible. They have to logically connect one point to the next. This isn't always easy. It's difficult for a reporter to piece everything together and still get across the impact of the event. Many good writers are bad reporters, because they can't conform to this way of writing. Even many good reporters find this artificial restriction a problem.

What's a problem for the reporter is good for us, though, because it provides us with a way to examine the author's argument. Every paragraph is a building block in the author's argument. Identify the main point of each paragraph, which most often is in the first sentence. Scribble that idea in the margin next to the paragraph. When you move to the next paragraph, identify its main idea. See how that relates to the main idea of the previous paragraph. Scribble that in the margin. Stringing together all your marginal comments should provide a map of the author's argument. For example, "illustrates author's point about small yapping dogs," "provides counterexample from dog lovers," "possible solution to the plague of small yapping dogs," and so on are possible marginal notes from an article on "Schnauzer Love."

At first, you can expect your summaries to be too long. Don't panic. (It's only a problem if your summaries are longer than the paragraph you're summarizing.) With practice, you'll get more concise. The best way to get really good at margin-noting and argument mapping is...to do it. Just DO it. A lot. Not only will this help you get more out of your journalistic reading, it gets your brain to condense information. This skill translates into faster reading rates and higher retention rates for all types of reading.

Exercise 11.2

Practice mapping and summarizing the following passage. Pay close attention to primary facts (as opposed to secondary facts). Use the margins for noting, and answer the questions after the passage using your marginal notes—try not to return to the passage once noted. You can check your answers on page 248.

THE 1996 CONVENTIONS/DEFYING HISTORY
Not since the Democrats held their riotous meeting there in 1968 has Chicago offered its hospitality to a big-party convention. That convention was supposed to draw the world's attention to the proud city of Mayor Richard M. Daley, then the Democratic Party's kingmaker. It turned into a well-televised brawl between the police and anti-Vietnam-war protestors, with fights along South Michigan Avenue in front of the convention headquarters. Now the Vietnam war is history, the Black Power movement has subsided, and Chicago's boosters think the city is overdue for a return to the political limelight.

Chicago's current Democratic mayor, Richard J. Daley, son of the late Richard M., is making bids for both the conventions at which the big parties will name their presidential candidates in 1996. He and Illinois' Republican governor, Jim Edgar, have set aside their quarrels to make a bipartisan pitch for the two events. The last city to win both nominating conventions was Miami, in 1972. The Chicago meetings would be held in the city's new United Center, a 21,500-seat, $175m arena due to open this August. It expects to do well with basketball and ice hockey during the winter, but would welcome the late-summer boost the parties' delegates would bring in 1996. If the city got both conventions, it could pull in more than $200m from spending by delegates. New York recouped from convention-related tax revenues the $28m it is reckoned to have spent on organizing the Democrats' 1992 meeting, and then earned $104m from convention visitors. Houston estimates it got $100m in direct spending from the Republican convention that year. Chicago thinks it should get the Democrats in 1996, anyway. David Wilhelm, chairman of the Democratic Party's national committee (DNC), which has the final say on the convention site, has lived in Chicago for years and is a former campaign adviser to Mayor Daley. The mayor's lawyer-brother, William Daley, was President Clinton's back-room ally in the fight to get the North American Free Trade Agreement through Congress. Another Chicago lawyer, John Schmidt, helped Mr. Clinton bring the GATT deal to its successful conclusion. He has yet to call in his political chips.

The DNC, which is also considering Los Angeles, San Antonio, Kansas City, and New Orleans, is expected to announce its choice by June. The Republicans' schedule is more sedate: they may not choose their site until the summer of 1995. The Republicans, however, have fixed the time of their convention: August 1996. The Democrats have yet to name their day. Since they hold the presidency, and the ruling party generally likes to meet after its rival, that could push 1996's political season into the last steamy days of summer.

Some Republicans are not keen on sharing a convention city with their rivals, saying that each party needs its own style and therefore its own site. But Chicago has a historical tilt toward the Republicans (it has been the site of 14 Republican conventions, as opposed to ten Democratic ones). And Governor Edgar's people point out that Illinois will be a key state in the 1996 presidential race, so holding the party's convention there might be a shrewd idea. They add that television and the press, which present the conventions to the nation, prefer to have both in the same city because it costs them less.

1. At the time this article was written, was the mayor of Chicago a Democrat or a Republican?

   _____

   _____

2. According to the article, which party was most likely to hold their convention first in 1996?

   _____

   _____

3. Give two reasons the Democrats considered holding their convention in Chicago.

   _____

   _____

4. Give two reasons the Republicans considered holding their convention in Chicago.

   _____

   _____

5. What was the relationship between the mayor of Chicago and the governor of Illinois at the time this article was written?

_____

_____

6. Why would Chicago have wanted to host either convention?

_____

_____

7. What factors worked against Chicago holding either convention?

_____

_____

Reflection

For any question you got wrong, go back and leave notes next to each answer choice indicating why it is correct or incorrect. It's important that you not only practice, but also reflect on your performance! This way, you'll see what issues give you trouble and gain a better understanding of how to improve.

Chapter 11 Summary

- Journalism is one of the most diverse fields of literature in both style and content.

- In any piece of journalism, the author presents an argument, though it may be subtle. Therefore, it's important to recognize the difference between fact and opinion, and which facts the author may have chosen in order to get you to feel or think a certain way.

- Be a skeptical reader. Don't accept what you read as truth right away. Analyze the piece, and figure out the argument that's being made and why. You can use argument-mapping, which means writing down the points the author makes in the order she makes them in order to get a sense of the article's structure.

- Use pre-reading to determine what you can expect from the piece and determine its main points. Pay attention to the title and any subheadings or emphasized quotes.

- If you need to skim an article, only read as far into any paragraph until you get its main idea. Then move on to the next paragraph.

CHAPTER 12

Poetry and Plays

"I've written some poetry I don't
understand myself."

—Carl Sandburg

The Basics

It's usually kind of an insult to call something "prosaic." That word can mean everyday, normal, or "basic" in the way that some young people today say "that's so basic." When something is basic or prosaic, it's kind of boring because it's rather predictable. Most of our experiences, with people and with texts, are kind of predictable. In the case of texts, this is because most of our experience is with something called prose, which gives "prosaic" its name.

When texts are not prosaic and basic, they might take other forms, such as poetry or drama. In all of these cases, authors present language arranged a certain way to achieve a desired effect. The form has something to do with what they are trying to say. Think of it this way: If a painter comes up with an image in her mind, she can realize that image in a number of ways:

> She can paint it on a canvas.
>
> She can tattoo it on her arm.
>
> She can tattoo it on someone else's arm.
>
> She can outline it on a sidewalk with pieces of dry bread.
>
> And so on...

The point is that the painter can achieve very different responses from people (and, in at least one case, birds) depending on how she chooses to present her image. *Prose*—writing in narrative form, usually in paragraphs and sentences—is the most common form of writing, just as canvas is the most common material on which to paint. Prose and canvas seem safer, more familiar and recognizable. But other means are certainly possible.

Poetry

What can you do with a poem? You can tell a story, show characters, explain a conflict, do much of what you can also do in prose, and then some, usually in a more condensed form. (Usually: *The Odyssey* and *The Iliad* are also poems.) There are three additional things that you can do when you write a poem.

One—the words can take a shape. In prose, you can tell the same thing in many different ways, but when someone looks at it on the page, they can't usually get an image, like words in the shape of a "V," or words that trail off like a person running out of breath. This does not mean that all poetry always uses its shape on a page to convey an idea. This just means that you should be aware and take a look. Some poetry makes use of its visual presentation to help convey meaning. Or as Marshall McLuhan once said, the medium *is* the message.

Two—poetry is inherently oral. It is a spoken medium. The sounds that emerge are sometimes as important as the exact words themselves. This doesn't mean just rhyme, although that can be a big part of it. Meter, rhythm, pauses, and timing all contribute to the feelings and thoughts a poem can evoke. This does not mean you absolutely must know what a caesura is, or what iambic pentameter specifically means. Try being aware of the cadence and the sound of the language. If you think you have no ear for sound and meaning, think of a song you like. The lyrics and the way they go with the music very much have something to do with poetry. This is as true in "Twinkle, Twinkle, Little Star" as well as the songs in the musical *Hamilton*.

Three—poetry removes much of the excess language of prose. Poetry is a condensed form. Every phrase, every word, every syllable, and every punctuation mark is intentional, with meaning and a relationship to those around it. They are there for a reason. Though you might not guess it from the typical idea of most poets' personalities, poetry is all business: Anything that doesn't work for the poem gets discarded. If something jumps out at you as unusual, or as a strange way of writing or punctuating, stop and ask yourself, "What is this doing? Why is this here?" Poetry is concentrated meaning. Everything in it contributes.

Now that you know all of this, reading poetry should feel less forbidding than it may have beforehand. If people write poems with these three things in mind, then you should read poems with these three things in mind. Ask yourself: "What does it look like? Is there a shape on the page? Or has the person decided to use an old form, referring to some earlier time?" Next, read the poem out loud. Ask: "What does it sound like? How do the words run together? Where are there pauses? What effect do they have?" Finally, look at the precise meaning of all the words. Much in the way that we theme-marked earlier, look for repeated or similar words. They usually spell out an underlying theme of the poem. The following is a poem by e.e. cummings (no, that is not a typo—he didn't capitalize his initials). He was a complicated and brilliant poet who is frequently misread and misunderstood. His poems may appear (at first) strange and inaccessible. But by asking these questions about his poem, you'll find that reading it is not so difficult after all.

> into the strenuous briefness
> Life:
> handorgans and April
> darkness, friends
>
> i charge laughing.
> Into the hair-thin tints
> of yellow dawn,
> into the women-coloured twilight
>
> i smilingly
> glide. I
> into the big vermilion departure
> swim, sayingly;
>
> (Do you think?) the
> i do, world
> is probably made
> of roses & hello:
>
> (of solongs and, ashes)

Question 1: What Does It Look Like on the Page?

There are four groups of four lines each, and it ends in a single line in parentheses. It starts with Life and April (spring), but also with darkness, and it ends with solongs (on our fifth read, we realized this might refer to statements like "so long" that one uses to say goodbye) and ashes (burnt remains of something, maybe roses, maybe something else). So, hmm, what about the number four? If April reminds you of spring, you can remember that there are four seasons of the year. Could the poem be partly about the movement from spring to winter? Does entertaining that idea let you reread it and think different thoughts this time? Can you consider a different hypothesis and read it again and think even different thoughts? Yes, you can. Maybe this is part of the point of poetry. Not to overwhelm you, but a number of political philosophers have talked about poetry as expressing the natural freedom of the human mind.

Question 2: What Does It Sound Like?

We know: it sounds strenuous, it sounds brief. But seriously, the lines are quite short, which helps you feel the huge difference between just line 1 and line 2. The punctuation gives you some clues about how long to pause between words, and that helps you feel the faster rhythm of some lines and the slower rhythm of other lines. There are also parentheses. How do those sound? We're not sure either, but if the parenthetical statements are private thoughts, maybe you could imagine hearing or speaking them more softly.

The middle stanzas (groups of lines) contain words that evoke visual and physical experiences. So cummings is using the sounds of language to get your ear to make your brain imagine several senses.

Question 3: How Are the Language and Structure Different from Typical Language Use?

In asking this question, you might begin to wonder about cummings' strange fourth stanza. It's definitely not "basic." Well, just rearrange the words a bit and consider this possibility: now, we have a question that reads "Do you think the world is probably made of roses and hello?" Do you think that life may be about love and beginnings? And we have an answer: "i do." But that's not the poet's final word. After his "i do" we have a concluding line, a "so long" to the reader, that reminds us that "hello" is at some point followed by "solongs," that "roses" are followed by "ashes." So this is cummings speaking in both cases. Maybe we have cummings's older beliefs in the centrality of hello and roses along with his newer beliefs in the inevitability of endings. And actually, considering this can help you reread the poem and see that, in fact, every stanza has beginnings and endings, greetings and departures.

Imagine Adele singing this poem. Nice, isn't it?

Now, only e.e. cummings really knew for sure what he meant here, and even then, maybe not. But for your purpose, which might be to be indelibly touched by the poem, or maybe just to quickly come up with an essay topic, you should responsibly use the freedom of your mind. That is, first of all, don't be afraid. Consider the possibility that everything is meaningful, and take your own best guess; follow your instincts. Don't be afraid to voice your ideas even without absolute certainty. (This is good training for being in the world in general.) So be free, but also be responsible. That is, don't be a jerk and claim that anyone can say anything about the meaning of the poem. Really? What if we said that the poem (published before 1962, when cummings died) was about the possibilities of communicating on Twitter in 2017? Would you really want to back us up here? No. This interpretation of poetry is just wrong. Which proves that some interpretations of poetry Are. Just. Wrong. If we said that the poem is about World War II, we'd be wrong in a different way. If we said it was about appreciating what life gives, even though everything changes and passes, we won't have said the final word on the subject, but we'd be much closer to being "right," a word which here means "relevant and interesting for other readers who care about their reading of the poem and who care about the meaning of words."

Exercise 12

Here's a poem for you to walk through on your own. Feel free to use the three questions discussed on pages 191–192 as a way of getting started. You can compare your analysis to ours on page 249.

Words

Axes
After whose stroke the wood rings,
And the echoes!
Echoes traveling
Off from the center like horses.

The sap
Wells like tears, like the
Water striving
To re-establish its mirror
Over the rock

That drops and turns,
A white skull,
Eaten by weedy greens.
Years later I
Encounter them on the road—

Words dry and riderless,
The indefatigable hoof-taps
While
From the bottom of the pool, fixed stars
Govern a life.

The Play's the Thing

A play, like a score of music, is usually meant to be performed, not just read. A play relies on people to bring it to life. So if you're reading a play, and it seems tough to follow, try reading it out loud. Sure, your roommates or your parents may wonder what's going on. But you'll understand the play better than they will, and who knows, maybe you will be discovered by an agent looking for someone to dub foreign films.

Why Plays?

A playwright writes for actors who are playing characters. Try to picture what you think each character looks like, where they are, and what they wear. This may help you get beyond some dialogue you don't particularly like. If you can find out the basic plot of the play before you pick it up, do that. Plays are not only about plot, but also about language and character. The plot is the skeleton that allows development of character and use of language. Even in a play like *Deathtrap*, which relies on surprises and trickery, each character's state of mind is more important than the external plot. This is true of classic plays as well. Let's look at *Hamlet*. A kid's father's ghost claims that he was murdered by his mother's new husband. The kid drives them nuts so they pay for their actions, and he's crazy too. Or maybe he's not. Oh, and he's the prince of Denmark. That's it. Is that why this play is a classic? Absolutely not. It's because of the language, and the extremes to which this situation drives the characters.

If you have the opportunity to see a play in addition to reading it, see it. Keep in mind that Hollywood and your local theater always change at least one important thing, so you shouldn't rely solely on seeing a play to get all you can out of it. The reason you should see a play is because it makes the words come alive. They move from the page to a character's mouth.

The Arc of Triumph

Plays generally (but not always—particularly from 1950 on) progress in an arc. What do we mean by *arc*? Basically, plays begin with a given situation and end with a modified situation. The play is about how they get from beginning to end, about what causes the change. The arc of the play, then, is that movement, from beginning, through conflict or change, to the end. If you're reading a book and you're pressed for time, you can read the first and last chapters to see this kind of change, and figure out the rest. In a play, it's the change itself that is the important thing. So you must understand the specifics. Why did things occur? How did the change occur? Who was for it? Who was against it? Who is affected by it? A good way to look at a play is to identify the following parts (don't worry if every play doesn't contain all these parts—it will have some of them):

- **The Prologue**—This is what is considered "normal life" for the characters. It is intended give you a snapshot of each character and quickly identify who they are and what their situation is.

- **The Conflict**—This is what is going to change the normal life of the characters presented. It can be the arrival of another character, the death of a character, an inheritance, a lawsuit, a robbery, even a ghost—almost anything that affects their way of life.

- **The Climax**—This is where the conflict is resolved in one way or another. The climax doesn't have to be the most dramatic moment in the play; it just has to be the moment after which nothing is the same again. In smash-up movies, the climax is usually the big car chase at the end. In plays, the climax can be any time the world is changed. In *King Lear,* for example, the climax comes right at the beginning when he divides his kingdom.

- **The Epilogue**—This is the new state of the world after the climax. It could be disastrous. It could be a change for the better (but not usually). The primary message of a play is usually found in comparing the epilogue to the prologue. Is the world better? Is the world worse? And do the characters have a future or not?

When you're reading a play, you should go through the text and find these spots. These sections are your most useful signposts. Use them to make the text more understandable and to enjoy the language more.

Chapter 12 Summary

- Literary genres like poetry and drama can achieve different effects and emotional responses than can prose works.

- When reading a poem, be aware that every aspect of it is intentional: the words, punctuation, syllables, and even the sound and shape.

- Read poems aloud to get their full effect. Pay attention to certain sounds or words that are repeated. Ask yourself:

    o What does the poem look like on the page?

    o What does the poem sound like?

    o How are the language and structure of the poem different from typical language use?

- Just like a musical score is meant to be played, plays are meant to be performed, not just read.

- Plays have a few basic parts: the prologue, the conflict, the climax, and the epilogue. When reading or viewing a play, it's important to understand how these four parts are connected and work together.

PART III

More Reading Practice

CHAPTER 13

Additional Reading Zones

> "The further you get away from yourself, the more challenging it is. Not to be in your comfort zone is great fun."
>
> —Benedict Cumberbatch

Reading Zone 13.1

Read the following passage and then answer the questions that follow. You can check your answers on page 249.

Don't think: write!

When we write, for whom do we write? Or as we would be more likely to ask, who do we write for? It sounds like an easy question to answer, and in some ways it is. But when it is applied to the matter of fiction, the logical answer—that we write for a specific audience—doesn't always work.

Each year I teach at one or more writers' workshops. I enjoy them for many reasons, not the least of which is the opportunity to meet other workshop leaders, often writers whose work I have long admired. Writing is a solitary profession, and a writers' conference gives us a chance to get together. Another reason I enjoy the workshops is that I am forced to articulate what I have learned about the techniques of the craft of fiction writing; it is easy to get forgetful and sloppy. Having to explain imagery, simile, metaphor, point of view, is a way to continue to teach myself as well as the people who have come to the workshop.

At one workshop, I talked, as usual, about all the hard work that precedes the writing of fiction. Often there is research to be done. For my Time Trilogy I had to immerse myself in the new physics: first, Einstein's theories of relativity and Planck's quantum theory for *A Wrinkle in Time*; then cellular biology and particle physics for *A Wind in the Door*; and astrophysics and non-linear theories of time for *A Swiftly Tilting Planet*. For *The Love Letters* I had to learn a great deal more about seventeenth-century Portuguese history than I needed or wanted to know, so that the small amount needed for the book would be accurate. Before, during, and after research, the writer needs to be thinking constantly about the characters, and the direction in which the novel seems to be moving.

Does the story have the Aristotelian beginning, middle, and end? How do the events of the novel relate to me, personally, in my own journey through life? What are my own particular concerns at the time of writing, and how should they affect—or not affect—the story? When I actually sit down to write, I stop thinking. While I am writing, I am listening to the story; I am not listening to myself. "But," a young woman in the class said in a horrified tone of voice, "my creative writing teacher says that we must keep the audience in mind at all times." That is undoubtedly true for the scientists writing an article that is expected to be understood by people who have little or no scientific background. The writer will have to keep simplifying scientific language, explaining technical terms. Keeping the audience in mind is probably valuable for reporting in newspapers and magazines. The reporter is writing for the average reader; language should be neither so bland as to be insulting, nor so technical as to demand special knowledge.

As for lawyers, I assume they have each other in mind at all times as they write. Certainly they don't have most of us in mind. Their grandiosity appalls me. In a movie contract, I was asked to grant the rights to my book to the producers, in perpetuity, throughout the universe. When I wrote in, "With the exception of Sagittarius and the Andromeda galaxy," it was accepted. Evidently the lawyers, who are writing to avoid litigation in a litigious world, did not anticipate a lawsuit from Sagittarius. Of course I am being grossly unfair to many lawyers; I come from a family of fine lawyers. But the language used in a will or a contract is indeed a special language, and it is not aimed at the reader who enjoys stories, the reader of fiction.

Whom, then, does the writer of fiction write for? It is only a partial truth to say that I write for myself, out of my own need, asking, whether I realize it or not, the questions I am asking in my own life. A truer answer is that I write for the book. "But why do you write for children?" I am often asked. And I answer truthfully that I don't. I haven't been a child for a long time, and if what I write doesn't appeal to me, at my age, it isn't likely to appeal to a child. I hope I will never lose the child within me, who has not lost her sense of wonder, of awe, of laughter. But I am not a child; I am a grown woman, learning about maturity as I move on in chronology.

A teacher, in introducing me to a class of seventh graders, said, "Miss L'Engle has made it in the children's field, and she is now trying to break into the adult market." I felt that I had better not explain to this teacher that I had no desire to break into the adult market and see my fiction in "adult bookstores."...I did explain that my first several books were regular trade novels, which means that they were marketed for a general audience, not for children. And I explained that when I have a book that I think will be too difficult for a general audience, then we will market it as a juvenile book. It is a great mistake to think that children are not capable of understanding difficult concepts in science or philosophy.

A book that has a young protagonist will likely be marketed as a children's book, regardless of content. Since adolescents are usually more willing than their elders to ask difficult questions, and to accept the fact that the questions don't have nice, tidy answers but lead on to more difficult questions, approximately half of my books have young protagonists. But while I am writing, I am not thinking of any audience at all. I am not even thinking about myself. I am thinking about the book. This does not imply anything esoteric. I do not pick up the pen and expect it to guide my hand, or put my fingers on the keyboard of the typewriter and expect the work to be done automatically. It is work. But it is focused work, and the focus is on the story, not on anything else. An example of the kind of focus I mean is a good doctor. The good doctor listens to the patient, truly listens, to what the patient says, does not say, is afraid to say, to body language, to everything that may give a clue as to what is wrong. The good doctor is so fully focused on the patient that personal self-consciousness has vanished. Such focused listening does not make the doctor—or any of the rest of us—less ourselves. In fact, such focused listening makes us more ourselves.

The same thing is true in listening to a story as we write it. It does not make us any less writers, this strange fact that we do not think about writing as we are writing; it makes us more writers.

1. What profession does the author of the passage liken to being a good writer?
   - (A) Lawyer
   - (B) Astronaut
   - (C) Therapist
   - (D) Doctor
   - (E) Physicist

2. Which of the following adjectives does the author use to characterize the profession of writing?
   - (A) Rigid
   - (B) Solitary
   - (C) Childish
   - (D) Noble
   - (E) Sloppy

3. A book written by the author of the passage is called
   - (A) *A Wrinkle in Space*
   - (B) *The Wind in Time*
   - (C) *A Door in Time*
   - (D) *A Swiftly Tilting Universe*
   - (E) *The Love Letters*

4. As defined in the passage, a "trade novel" is
   - (A) one specifically written for children
   - (B) one written for a specific trade
   - (C) one marketed for children
   - (D) one marketed for a specific trade
   - (E) one marketed for a general audience

5. According to the passage, all of the following are things the author explains to her creative writing classes EXCEPT
   (A) simile
   (B) metaphor
   (C) imagery
   (D) resonance
   (E) point of view

6. The author has had to resist the label of being a(n)
   (A) children's author
   (B) adult author
   (C) trade author
   (D) popular author
   (E) esoteric author

7. The author would most likely DISAGREE with which of the following statements?
   (A) Writing should be performed with the work in mind, not the audience.
   (B) Teaching writing can be a valuable experience for the teacher.
   (C) Young protagonists are often mistakenly viewed as childish.
   (D) Difficult concepts should be written about with adults in mind, not children.
   (E) When one is writing well, the work will be focused.

8. Her annotation of the contract selling her rights, excluding those rights in Sagittarius and the Andromeda Galaxy, was meant to be
   (A) detached
   (B) ironic
   (C) angered
   (D) political
   (E) sophomoric

9. For whom does the author write?
   (A) The work
   (B) Her audience
   (C) Her protagonists
   (D) Her children
   (E) Children of all countries

10. Which of the following summarizes the main point of the passage?
    (A) Work that contains children should not be assumed to be juvenile literature.
    (B) Whereas certain types of writers write for an audience, the fiction writer should write for the work.
    (C) Whereas certain types of writers write for an audience, the journalistic writer should write for the work.
    (D) Whereas certain doctors who listen are good, so are certain writers who listen to the story in their heads.
    (E) To assume that writing is an easy task is false.

Reading Zone 13.2

Read the following passage and then answer the questions that follow. You can check your answers on page 250.

To the red country and part of the gray country of Oklahoma, the last rains came gently, and they did not cut the scarred earth. The plows crossed and recrossed the rivulet marks. The last rains lifted the corn quickly and scattered weed colonies and grass along the sides of the roads so that the gray country and the dark red country began to disappear under a green cover. In the last part of May the sky grew pale and the clouds that had hung in high puffs for so long in the spring were dissipated. The sun flared down on the growing corn day after day until a line of brown spread along the edge of each green bayonet. The clouds appeared, and went away, and in a while they did not try any more. The weeds grew darker green to protect themselves, and they did not spread anymore. The surface of the earth crusted, a thin hard crust, and as the sky became pale, so the earth became pale, pink in the red country and white in the gray country. In the water-cut gullies the earth dusted down in dry little streams. Gophers and ant lions started small avalanches. And as the sharp sun struck day after day, the leaves of the young corn became less stiff and erect; they bent in a curve at first, and then, as the central ribs of strength grew weak, each leaf tilted downward. Then it was June, and the sun shone more fiercely. The brown lines on the corn leaves widened and moved in on the central ribs. The weeds frayed and edged back toward their roots. The air was thin and the sky more pale; and every day the earth paled.

In the roads where the teams moved, where the wheels milled the ground and the hooves of the horses beat the ground, the dirt crust broke and the dust formed. Every moving thing lifted the dust into the air; a walking man lifted a thin layer as high as his waist, and a wagon lifted the dust as high as the fence tops, and an automobile boiled a cloud behind it. The dust was long in settling back again. When June was half gone, the big clouds moved up out of Texas and the Gulf, high heavy clouds, rainheads. The men in the fields looked up at the clouds and sniffed at them and half wet fingers up to sense the wind. And the horses were nervous while the clouds were up. The rainheads dropped a little spattering and hurried on up to some other country. Behind them the sky was pale again and the sun flared. In the dust there were drop craters where the rain had fallen, and there were clean splashes on the corn, and that was all.

A gentle wind followed the rain clouds, driving them on northward, a wind that softly clashed the drying corn. A day went by and the wind increased, steady, unbroken by gusts. The dust from the roads fluffed up and spread out and fell on the weeds beside the fields, and fell into the fields a little way. Now the wind grew strong and hard and it worked at the rain crust in the corn fields. Little by little the sky was darkened by the mixing dust, and the wind felt over the earth, loosened the dust and carried it away. The wind grew stronger. The rain crust broke and the dust lifted up out of the fields and drove gray plumes into the air like sluggish smoke. The corn threshed the wind and made a dry, rushing sound. The finest dust did not settle back to earth now, but disappeared into the darkening sky. The wind grew stronger, whisked under stones, carried up straws and old leaves, and even little clods, marking its course as it sailed across the fields. The air and the sky darkened and through them the sun shone redly, and there was a raw sting in the air. During a night the wind raced faster over the land, dug cunningly among the rootlets of the corn, and the corn fought the wind with its weakened leaves until the roots were freed by the prying wind and then each stalk settled wearily sideways toward the earth and pointed the direction of the wind.

The dawn came, but not day. In the gray sky a red sun appeared, a dim red circle that gave a little light, like dust; and as that day advanced, the dusk slipped back toward darkness, and the wind cried and whimpered over the fallen corn.

Men and women huddled in their houses, and they tied handkerchiefs over their noses when they went out, and wore goggles to protect their eyes. When the night came again it was black night, for the stars could not pierce the dust to get down, and the window lights could not even spread beyond their own yards. Now the dust was evenly mixed with the air, an emulsion of dust and air. Houses were shut tight, and cloth wedged around doors and windows, but the dust came in so thinly that it could not be seen in the air, and it settled like pollen on the chairs and tables, on the dishes. The people brushed it from their shoulders. Little lines of dust lay at the door sills.

In the middle of that night the wind passed on and left the land quiet. The dust-filled air muffled sound more completely than fog does. The people, lying in their beds, heard the wind stop. They awakened when the rushing wind was gone. They lay quietly and listened deep into the stillness. Then the roosters crowed, and their voices were muffled, and the people stirred restlessly in their beds and wanted the morning. They knew it would take a long time for the dust to settle out of the air. In the morning the dust hung like fog, and the sun was as red as ripe new blood. All day the dust sifted down from the sky, and the next day it sifted down. An even blanket covered the earth. It settled on the corn, piled up on the tops of the fence posts, piled up on the wires; it settled on roofs, blanketed the weeds and trees. The people came out of their houses and smelled the hot stinging air and covered their noses from it. And the children came out of the houses, but they did not run or shout as they would have done after a rain. Men stood by their fences and looked at the ruined corn, drying fast now, only a little green showing through the film of dust. The men were silent and they did not move often. And the women came out of the houses to stand beside their men—to feel whether this time the men would break. The women studied the men's faces secretly, for the corn could go, as long as something else remained. The children stood near by, drawing figures in the dust with bare toes, and the children sent exploring senses out to see whether men and women would break. The children pecked at the faces of the men and women, and then drew careful lines in the dust with their toes. Horses came to the watering troughs and nuzzled the water to clear the surface dust. After a while the faces of the watching men lost their bemused perplexity and became hard and angry and resistant. Then the women knew that they were safe and there was no break. Then they asked, What'll we do? And the men replied, I don't know. But it was all right. The women knew it was all right, and the watching children knew it was all right. Women and children knew deep in themselves that no misfortune was too great to bear if their men were whole. The women went into the houses to their work and the children began to play, but cautiously at first. As the day went forward the sun became less red. It flared down on the dust-blanketed land. The men sat in the doorways of their houses; their hands were busy with sticks and little rocks. The men sat still—thinking—figuring.

1. The characters in the passage are concerned with what natural phenomenon?
   (A) Storms
   (B) Drought
   (C) Animal death
   (D) Poverty
   (E) Eclipse

2. An image that appears throughout the passage is
   (A) dust
   (B) redness
   (C) clouds
   (D) wind
   (E) all of the above

3. The tone of the passage is
   (A) journalistic
   (B) textbook-like
   (C) novelistic
   (D) biblical
   (E) ominous

4. The attitude of the passage is
   (A) optimistic
   (B) pessimistic
   (C) neutral
   (D) conciliatory
   (E) hateful

5. The image of the men in the doorway at the end is most likely meant to inspire
   (A) hope
   (B) despair
   (C) ridicule
   (D) anger
   (E) love

6. The phrase "[t]he dawn came but no day" means that
   (A) there was an eclipse
   (B) the sun rose but no light could be seen
   (C) the sun was clear in the morning, but became more clouded by noon
   (D) the day was blotted out by fog
   (E) the smoke from the fires covered up the sun

7. This passage would be most appropriate as
   (A) the opening to a novel
   (B) the closing of a novel
   (C) the opening of a short story
   (D) the closing of a short story
   (E) an entire short story

8. Which of the following is given human attributes throughout the passage?
   (A) The clouds
   (B) The corn
   (C) The weeds
   (D) The wind
   (E) All of the above

9. The term "rainheads" as used in the passage means
   (A) people who keep looking for signs of rain
   (B) Gulf weather
   (C) heavy clouds
   (D) light sprinkling
   (E) dust that settles before rain

10. The dust settling like "pollen" in the houses is meant to be
    (A) a painful and ironic reminder of the land's infertility
    (B) a promise of a more fruitful future when the dust will pass
    (C) a powerful symbol of the possibilities of life in the house, but not out of the house
    (D) a brutal, killing gesture destroying all hope for the future
    (E) all of the above

Reading Zone 13.3

Read the following editorial from the early 1990s about Kim Il Sung, who ruled in North Korea until 1994. Remember our strategies for reading journalistic writing, such as distinguishing between fact and opinion and mapping an argument. You can check your answers to the questions on page 251.

Kim Il Sung, the North Korean dictator—redeemer to his people, and madman with a bomb to almost everyone else—sits in isolation in his capital, Pyongyang, letting the world guess what he is thinking. He is eighty-one years old and affects the trappings of semiretirement. He wears Panama hats and color-coordinated outfits. He hunts wild boar from a safe distance, with rifles fitted with telescopic sights. He is said to have relinquished the everyday affairs of state to his son and heir, Kim Jong Il, who is fifty-one. All that is missing is a photograph with grandchildren. He is believed to have at least two.

The affectation is deceptive. Forty-eight years after Stalin set Kim Il Sung on his throne, he remains an object of fear, and perhaps never more so than now. This is a considerable achievement for a ruler whose economy is believed to be in such ruin that his people are encouraged to eat just two meals a day. Kim Il Sung inspires fear not only because he may possess one or two nuclear weapons but also because he has made the world believe he would not hesitate to use them. Through the fall and winter, the United States has been trying to get North Korea to allow inspections of seven sites where bombs may be being made. Negotiators have trod warily, first hunting at confrontation and then backing off, the better not to provoke him.

A deal may be near—one in which the North Koreans will allow International Atomic Energy Agency inspectors to visit those seven sites but not two additional sites where inspectors suspect they might find evidence of bomb production. Satellite surveillance has its limits; the I.A.E.A. is demanding on-site inspections. The North Koreans, in return for complying with terms that they had in fact agreed to in 1985, will win the suspension of the United

Reading Smart

States-South Korea war games known as Team Spirit, which usually begin in late winter. And, more important, the North Koreans will force the Americans, whom they blame and despise for splitting Korea at the end of the Second World War, to negotiate the future of diplomatic relations between North Korea and the United States directly, and not in tandem with the South Koreans whom the North Koreans dismiss as American puppets.

But those who have watched Kim Il Sung over the years don't expect the crisis to end here. This confrontation with the West, they feel, is just the beginning. There is a growing suspicion that after the North Koreans agree to inspections they will contrive to make the visits difficult, if not impossible. The North Koreans are considered capable of reversing themselves once the inspectors arrive, perhaps barring entry to some of the sites, or maintaining that they never agreed to inspections at the very places specified in the agreement. Kim Il Sung has been waiting a long time for the moment when his powerful enemies—the Americans, in particular—are compelled to accept him as the leader of a nation that matters.

For decades, Kim Il Sung endured as a journalistic chestnut: the lunatic who presided over the world's most bizarre and longest-lasting cult of personality. North Korea was an Orwellian nightmare—a source of stories of a robotic people wearing Kim Il Sung pins, chanting his name, holding up colored placards to generate his likeness along the length of Kim Il Sung Stadium, and extolling the manifold accomplishments of the Great Leader and his son, the Dear Leader. Then the North Koreans would hold the crew of a captured American spy ship for eleven months, as they did after seizing the *U.S.S. Pueblo*, in 1968; or blow up half the South Korean Cabinet, as they did in 1983, in Rangoon; or blow up a South Korean airliner, as they did in 1987. For a while, at least, the eye-rolling would stop, and people in Washington, Seoul, Tokyo, and every other capital who felt themselves threatened by the angry whims of Kim Il Sung would once again try to determine just who it was they were dealing with.

The task was not easy. Although North Korea has diplomatic relations with more than a hundred countries, it
has effectively cut itself off from most of the world. Visitors find their tours and their access tightly limited and
closely monitored. Diplomats who have spent years in
Pyongyang tell of never visiting a North Korean home, or
even having a candid conversation with a North Korean.
The word that recurs when they speak of that posting
is "irrational." I have never met Kim Il Sung. Though I
have been to South Korea many times, I have never been
granted permission to visit the North. American journalists
visit North Korea on rare occasions; usually, the visit is
arranged for a group and coincides with a showcase event,
like Kim Il Sung's birthday. He almost never grants these
visitors an interview. He spoke with the *New York Times*
and the *Washington Post* for the first, and last, time in
1972. It has been tempting, then, to see Kim Il Sung
only in terms of threatening bombast, the vulgarity of his
cult, the monuments he has ordered built to preserve his
likeness for eternity. But to do that is to underestimate his
cunning. Kim Il Sung has always known what he wanted
for himself and for the nation he created in his own image.
He wanted the powerful countries to come to him, and to
treat him and his small nation as an equal. And, because
he has been willing to take his nation time and again to
the brink of disaster, to risk war with the United States,
he has made his enemies dread him. Now, to the world's
discomfort and chagrin, he is on the verge of realizing his
vainglorious dream.

1. According to the passage, the picture of Kim Il Sung as an
   uninvolved, relaxed man is
   (A) exaggerated
   (B) accurate
   (C) difficult to believe
   (D) a complete lie
   (E) an enticing image

2. The annual military exercise between South Korea and the United States was known as
   - (A) the I.A.E.A.
   - (B) the Pyongyang Conflict
   - (C) the Wargames
   - (D) the Winter Games
   - (E) the Team Spirit

3. According to the passage, all of the following are attributed to the North Koreans EXCEPT
   - (A) seizing of the *U.S.S. Pueblo*
   - (B) raiding the South Korean border for supplies
   - (C) blowing up a South Korean airliner
   - (D) blowing up half the South Korean cabinet.
   - (E) holding American soldiers captive for eleven months

4. According to the passage, the economic state of affairs in North Korea is considered
   - (A) dire
   - (B) recovering
   - (C) booming
   - (D) pre-industrial
   - (E) industrial

5. Kim Il Sung's attitude toward war can best be described as
   - (A) cavalier
   - (B) brinksmanship
   - (C) reluctance
   - (D) recalcitrance
   - (E) silent

6. The author would most likely DISAGREE with which of the following statements?
    (A)   Kim II Sung remains a leader worth fearing.
    (B)   Kim Jong II is not as powerful as Kim II Sung.
    (C)   The on-site nuclear inspections will most likely, under the I.A.E.A., go smoothly.
    (D)   Kim II Sung is unlikely to grant another Western interview.
    (E)   Kim II Sung is a smart, albeit difficult, man.

7. The North Koreans despise the Americans because of
    (A)   the warlike posture the United States has held toward dictatorships
    (B)   the economic stability of the United States
    (C)   resentment over the splitting of Korea after World War II
    (D)   resentment over the colonization of Korea in the 1950s
    (E)   the growing suspicion over nuclear rearmament

8. As described in the passage, the term "journalistic chestnut" means
    (A)   reporter's enigma
    (B)   investigative riddle
    (C)   reporter's comestibles
    (D)   investigative prize
    (E)   investigative power

9. The tone of the passage can best be described as
    (A)   threatening
    (B)   jocular
    (C)   objective
    (D)   warning
    (E)   occluding

10. According to the passage, tours to North Korea can be best described as
    (A) difficult and unimpressive
    (B) awkward and unenlightened
    (C) ignorant and ill-considered
    (D) limited and unrevealing
    (E) enlightening and frightening

Reading Zone 13.4

Read the following passage and then answer the questions that follow. You can check your answers on page 252.

Reflecting the developments in religion and philosophy, much Hellenistic culture was cosmopolitan and urbane, although some was individualistic and specialized. Above all, the Hellenistic age was a time when Greek culture spread through much of the inhabited world. It went to Asia, northern Africa, and eventually to Italy and the West. So firmly did it take root that it prevailed in Asia until the Arabs swept all before them in the seventh and eighth centuries C.E. It retained its dominance in the Byzantine Empire, and much of it was introduced by the Romans into the lands around the western Mediterranean.

There was some reciprocity in the process because the Greeks learned from the people they conquered; never, however, did the eastern cultures supplant the Greek. Hellenistic culture was a modified continuation of the Hellenic. Its chief characteristics were more individualism, a greater emphasis on man and nature, less idealism, and more realism. Knowledge became more specialized. Less often did thinkers concern themselves with all knowledge, as did Plato and Aristotle, but rather they concentrated on some area of knowledge.

The most enduring contributions of Hellenistic culture were made in science, generally by scientists patronized by the Hellenistic monarchs. In mathematics Euclid (c. 300 B.C.E.) developed geometry which he explained in his book the Elements. Hipparchus (c. 150 B.C.E.) invented trigonometry for his measurements of the earth and his astronomical calculations. He supported the geocentric theory which triumphed over the heliocentric theory of Aristarchus of Samos (c. 275 B.C.E.). Eratosthenes (276–196 B.C.E.) projected a map of the earth with lines of longitude and latitude and calculated the circumference of the world to within two hundred miles of the exact figure. The gifted Archimedes of Syracuse (287–212 B.C.E.) discovered specific gravity, explained the movement of heavenly bodies, and made marvelous mechanical inventions. He even did elementary calculus and solved the value of pi.

Stimulated by the vast conquests and the new lands and peoples they saw, other thinkers did good work in geography and botany. The excellent achievements in medicine helped to relieve human suffering, to improve medical care, and to prevent disease. Studying the human anatomy, Herophilus (c. 300 B.C.E.) identified the functions of the brain and nervous system and showed the role of the arteries in the circulation of blood. In this period the science of physiology began.

Scholarship flourished also in the humanities, which were supported by the Hellenistic monarchies, especially the Ptolemaic at Alexandria. Since Greek was the universal language of the Hellenistic age, cultivated scholars studied its construction and wrote grammars on it. Others worked at literary criticism and rhetoric. Great libraries developed at Alexandria, Pergamum, Rhodes, and Antioch. In the museum at Alexandria, scholars were subsidized by the Ptolemies just to "do scholarship." Although Hellenistic literature did not rival the excellence achieved in the fifth and fourth centuries B.C.E., it retained a vitality and the ability to develop new forms and themes for expressing the feeling of men whose sensibilities and tastes had been altered by the changes in politics, economics, science, philosophy, and religion.

The poet Callimachus (c. 250 B.C.E.), for a time head of the library at Alexandria, popularized the short epic dealing with mythological themes not used previously by poets. He engaged in a bitter literary feud with Apollonius of Rhodes (c. 210 B.C.E.) who adhered to the style of the long Homeric epic and who composed the immensely popular *Argonautica* with its tale of Jason and his quest for the Golden Fleece. Callimachus, after reading this poem, made his famous comment: "A big book, a big evil." The *Argonautica*, however, is still a favorite, whereas the short epics of Callimachus have not enjoyed such success.

As a protest against the more complex urban life, Theocritus of Sicily (c. third century B.C.E.) wrote pastoral idylls praising the rural life with its shepherd, flocks, and natural, bucolic scenes. Unfortunately only one complete play and fragments of others by the playwright Menander (342–290 B.C.E.) are extant, but they show that he created a new form of comedy and was a worthy continuator of Aristophanes. Meander portrayed life and its manners rather than some general incident or theme. His insights into ordinary people and his reflections on life are indicative of the realism and cynicism that, in contrast to the Hellenic period, pervaded the Hellenistic Age. His observation "We live not as we will, but as we can," reveals the contemporary view of life. Meander became a model for later Roman comedy and inspired the comedies of Moliere in the seventeenth century.

There was no history in the Hellenistic age to equal that of Herodotus or Thucydides, but the *Histories of Polybius* (205–125 B.C.E.), who wrote about Rome from 266 to 146 B.C.E., have been acknowledged in all ages as great history. Originally a Greek politician, Polybius became a prisoner of the Romans in 168 B.C.E. and was taken to Rome. There he soon became a friend of cultivated Romans, among them the general, Scipio Africanus. The perspective of Polybius was later widened by visits to lands overseas under Roman rule. He became an enthusiastic admirer of Rome and decided to write a history that would attempt to explain why the Romans became the masters of the Mediterranean world in fifty-three years. Like Thucydides, Polybius was not content merely to describe historical events; he wanted to know why events occurred. His analysis of why Rome was so successful in politics and military affairs is still largely accepted by historians. His theory that history moves in cycles has long influenced historians interested in the rise and decline of states and civilizations.

1. How does the passage characterize Hellenistic culture?
   - (A) Individualistic and specialized
   - (B) Cosmopolitan and urbane
   - (C) Religious and philosophical
   - (D) Pastoral and bucolic
   - (E) Plebian and choleric

2. All of the following are characteristic of Hellenistic culture EXCEPT
   - (A) a lesser emphasis on man
   - (B) a greater emphasis on nature
   - (C) a greater degree of individualism
   - (D) a lesser degree of idealism
   - (E) an enhanced sense of realism

3. Who wrote the *Argonautica*?
   - (A) Homer
   - (B) Calimachus
   - (C) Archimedes
   - (D) Apollonius
   - (E) Meander

4. According to the passage, all of the following were achievements of Archimedes EXCEPT
   - (A) elementary calculus
   - (B) advances in geometry
   - (C) the discovery of specific gravity
   - (D) the invention of mechanical devices
   - (E) an explanation of the movement of heavenly bodies

5. One of the famous libraries of the Greek civilization was located in
   (A) Pergamum
   (B) Athens
   (C) Sparta
   (D) Luxandra
   (E) Antioch

6. According to the passage, Greek culture spread to all of the following places EXCEPT
   (A) Asia
   (B) the Middle East
   (C) Northern Africa
   (D) Western Europe
   (E) Italy

7. Who wrote the *Histories*?
   (A) Polybius
   (B) Herotodous
   (C) Thucydidies
   (D) Scipio Africanus
   (E) Aesop

8. According to the passage, which best describes the development of knowledge in the Hellenistic era?
   (A) More generalized
   (B) More specialized
   (C) More rational
   (D) More mystical
   (E) Less accurate

9. Which of the following in use today were developed during the Hellenistic era?
   (A) The idea of history as cyclical
   (B) The use of maps for navigation
   (C) The geocentric theory
   (D) All of the above
   (E) None of the above

10. All of the following were Hellenistic figures EXCEPT
   (A) Euclid
   (B) Hipparchus
   (C) Aristotle
   (D) Eratosthenes
   (E) Archimedes of Syracuse

Reading Zone 13.5

Read the following passage and then answer the questions that follow. You can check your answers on page 253.

My first evening in Hollywood. It was so typical that I almost thought it had been arranged for me. It was by sheer chance, however, that I found myself rolling up to the home of a millionaire in a handsome black Packard. I had been invited to dinner by a perfect stranger. I didn't even know my host's name. Nor do I know it now.

The first thing which struck me, on being introduced all around, was that I was in the presence of wealthy people, people who were bored to death and who were all, including the octogenarians, already three sheets to the wind. The host and hostess seemed to take pleasure in acting as bartenders. It was hard to follow the conversation because everybody was talking at cross purposes. The important thing was to get an edge on before sitting down to the table. One old geezer who had recently recovered from a horrible automobile accident was having his fifth old fashioned—he was proud of the fact, proud that he could swill it like a youngster even though he was partially crippled. Every one thought he was a marvel. There wasn't an attractive woman about, except the one who had brought me to the place. The men looked like businessmen, except for one or two who looked like aged strike breakers. There was one fairly young couple, in their thirties, I should say. The husband was a typical go-getter, one of those ex-football players who go in for publicity or insurance or the stock market, some clean all-American pursuit in which you run no risk of soiling your hands. He was a graduate of some Eastern University and had the intelligence of a high-grade chimp.

That was the set-up. When every one had been properly soused dinner was announced. We seated ourselves at a long table, elegantly decorated, with three or four glasses beside each plate. The ice was abundant, of course. The service began, a dozen flunkies buzzing at your elbow like horse flies. There was a surfeit of everything: a poor man would have had sufficient with the hors-d'oeuvres alone.

As they ate, they became more discursive, more argumentative. An elderly thug in a tuxedo who had the complexion of a boiled lobster was railing against labor agitators. He had a religious train, much to my amazement, but it was more like Torquemada's than Christ's. President Roosevelt's name almost gave him an apoplectic fit. Roosevelt, Bridges, Stalin, Hitler—they were all in the same class to him. That is to say, they were anathema. He had an extraordinary appetite which served, it seemed, to stimulate his adrenal glands. By the time he had reached the meat course he was talking about hanging being too good for some people. The hostess, meanwhile, who was seated at his elbow, was carrying on one of those delightful inconsequential conversations with the person opposite her. She had left some beautiful dachshunds in Biarritz, or was it Sierra Leone, and to believe her, she was greatly worried about them. In times like these, she was saying, people forget about animals. People can be so cruel, especially in time of war. Why, in Peking the servants had run away and left her with forty trunks to pack—it was outrageous. It was so good to be back in California. God's own country, she called it. She hoped the war wouldn't spread to America. Dear me, where was one to go now? You couldn't feel safe anywhere, except in the desert perhaps.

The ex-football player was talking to someone at the far end of the table in a loud voice. It happened to be an Englishwoman and he was insulting her roundly and openly for daring to arouse sympathy for the English in this country. "Why don't you go back to England?" he shouted at the top of his voice. "What are you doing here? You're a menace. We're not fighting to hold the British Empire together. You're a menace. You ought to be expelled from the country."

The woman was trying to say that she was not English but Canadian, but she couldn't make herself heard above the din. The octogenarian, who was now sampling the champagne, was talking about the automobile accident. Nobody was paying any attention to him. Automobile accidents were too common—everyone at the table had been in a smash-up at one time or another. One doesn't make a point about such things unless one is feeble-minded.

The hostess was clapping her hands frantically—she wanted to tell us a little story about an experience she had in Africa once, on one of her safaris.

"Oh, can that!" shouted the football player. "I want to find out why this great country of ours, in the most crucial moment..."

"Shut up!" screamed the hostess. "You're drunk." "That makes no difference," came his booming voice. "I want to know if we're all hundred percent Americans—and if not why not. I suspect that we have some traitors in our midst," and because I hadn't been taking part in any of the conversation he gave me a fixed, drunken look which was intended to make me declare myself. All I could do was smile.

1. Who says "you couldn't feel safe anywhere, except in the desert perhaps"?
   (A) The author
   (B) The narrator
   (C) The host
   (D) The hostess
   (E) The football player

2. What is the narrator's tone?
   (A) Ironic
   (B) Objective
   (C) Impressed
   (D) Spiteful
   (E) Disapproving

3. When would be the appropriate era for this piece?
   (A) The Spanish Inquisition
   (B) World War II
   (C) Pre-World War II
   (D) Post-World War II
   (E) Vietnam

4. What was a subject of discussion prior to dinner?
   - (A) America's entry into the war
   - (B) The octogenarian's condition
   - (C) Model trains
   - (D) Anathema
   - (E) The hostess's African safari

5. Why did the football player accuse the narrator of being a traitor?
   - (A) The narrator supported Roosevelt.
   - (B) The narrator did not support Roosevelt.
   - (C) The narrator advocated support for the British.
   - (D) The narrator remained silent.
   - (E) The football player didn't accuse him.

6. To whom did the octogenarian tell the story of his accident?
   - (A) The old accident victim
   - (B) The football player
   - (C) The football player's wife
   - (D) The narrator
   - (E) No one at all

7. According to the passage, the hostess has never traveled to
   - (A) Biarritz
   - (B) Africa
   - (C) Germany
   - (D) Peking
   - (E) Sierra Leone

8. What topic "stimulated the adrenal glands" of one of the guests?
   - (A) Hitler and Stalin
   - (B) Roosevelt and Bridges
   - (C) The main course
   - (D) America's entry into the war
   - (E) Alcohol

9. How long had the author been in Hollywood on the evening discussed?
   (A)   He had lived there for over ten years.
   (B)   He was spending his first night in Hollywood.
   (C)   He was spending his third night in Hollywood.
   (D)   He had lived there for one year.
   (E)   He had lived there for three years.

10. Which of the following best describes the author's attitude toward the other guests?
   (A)   Comical
   (B)   Respectful
   (C)   Dislike
   (D)   Anathema
   (E)   Friendly

Reflection

For any question you got wrong, go back and leave notes next to each answer choice indicating why it is correct or incorrect. It's important that you not only practice, but also reflect on your performance! This way, you'll see what issues give you trouble and gain a better understanding of how to improve.

Answer Key for Exercises and Reading Zones

Chapter 1

Exercise 1

1. fast	6. fast	11. medium
2. medium	7. slow	12. slow
3. fast	8. medium	13. medium
4. medium	9. fast	14. fast
5. slow	10. slow	15. medium

Reading Zone 1

1. According to the passage, what does "internally democratic" mean?
   (D) The election of delegates is done democratically.

2. The main point of the passage is to
   (D) show that internal democracy does not necessarily ensure accurate representation

3. Barry Goldwater's defeat can be ascribed to
   (E) the capture of the Republican platform by extremists

4. Which statement would the author most likely agree with?
   (D) Political parties can be likened to businesses in their organization.

5. According to the passage, a sign of health in the political parties is
   (A) the expanding participation in presidential primaries

Chapter 2

Reading Zone 2

1. According to the passage, Henry Hill's arrest was described by police as
   (D) a "prize beyond measure"

2. Why was Hill's arrest so important?
   (D) He had information on many unsolved crimes.

3. Why was it so easy for Hill to "disappear"?
   (B) There was little legal evidence of his existence.

4. Which best describes Hill's position in the mob?
   (C) Low but knowledgeable

5. According to the passage, Paul Vario
   (C) raised Henry Hill

Chapter 3

Exercise 3

1. intimate	slow	long time
2. passing	fast	til tomorrow
3. casual	medium	til tomorrow
4. passing	fast	til tomorrow
5. intimate	slow	long time
6. casual	medium	for life
7. passing	fast	til tomorrow
8. intimate	slow	long time
9. intimate	medium	for life
10. casual	medium	til tomorrow
11. passing	fast	til tomorrow
12. intimate	fast	til tomorrow

Reading Zone 3

1. The primary subject of the passage can best be summarized as
   (A) short story writers of the Twenties

2. Anderson's stories could best be described as
   (C) revolutionary

3. According to the passage, what makes secondary writers important?
   (D) The competition improves writers in general.

4. How do most readers feel about Hemingway's artistic progress?
   (E) Over time, he began to flourish within the boundaries of the short story.

5. The "deluge" referred to in the passage means
   (E) the overwhelming emergence

Chapter 4

Reading Zone 4.1

1. According to the passage, one painter from the "urban realist" school was
   (E) Isabel Bishop

2. According to the passage, in the 1930s, abstract art was seen as
   (E) counter to American regionalism

3. American Scene painters were characterized by
   (C) representing American values

4. In 1931, the director of the Art Students League was
   (D) John Sloan

5. The "artificial double standard" mention in the passage refers to
   (A) the difference between standards of judgment for European art and American art

6. According to the passage, one artist who advocated a return to earlier values was
   (B) Thomas Hart Benton

7. The best word to describe America in the 1930s would be
   (A) reactionary

8. According to the passage, one response to industrialization was
   (B) a conservative movement in art

9. According to the passage, Stuart Davis was a representative of
   (E) industrialization accepted by art

10. The best choice for title of the above passage would be
    (A) "The Thirties in Art: Reaction and Rebellion"

Reading Zone 4.2

1. According to the passage, the action initially responsible for the downfall of President Nixon was
   (B) the Watergate break-in

2. The term "smoking gun," as used in the passage, implies
   (D) information which proved Nixon's culpability

3. The name of the *second* special prosecutor was
   (A) Leon Jaworski

4. The purpose of the initial break-in at the Watergate Hotel was to
   (E) plant listening devices

5. The special senate committee was headed by
   (B) Sam Ervin

6. Which of the following, if true, most supports the author's position?
   (C) Richard Nixon grew up insecure and unsure of his position in life.

7. Who, according to the passage, was most responsible for the downfall of President Nixon?
   (E) Richard Nixon

8. Which member of the Nixon advisers was integral in the planning of the Bay of Pigs invasion?
   (D) E. Howard Hunt

9. The title *Breach of Faith* refers to
   (A) the disregard of the president for the electorate

10. The "Saturday Night Massacre" mentioned in the passage refers to
    (C) the firing of Archibald Cox and the special prosecutors

Reading Zone 4.3

1. The tone of the author is best described as
   (A) jocular

2. The author's "elf name" is
   (E) Crumpet

3. According to the passage, what was the author's reason for wanting to be an elf?
   (E) He thought it the most ridiculous job in the world.

4. According to the passage, why was he chosen to be an elf by management?
   (D) He was the right physical type.

5. All of the following are elf positions at Macy's EXCEPT
   (A) Escalator Elf

6. The job the author received was
   (B) Santa Elf

7. The author's knickers were
   (C) velvet green

8. The author can best be described as
   (D) an unenthusiastic elf

9. Why did the woman next to the author at his second interview want to be an elf?
   (E) She never really answered the question.

10. This piece would most likely be found in
    (A) a diary

Chapter 5

Exercise 5

1. Ninja Charles kicked a wall, died when the roof fell.
2. Stan Lee's Iron Man unexpectedly became a hero to the physically disabled.
3. Ethan was crazy mad, bolted from the party.
4. Drunk Uncle Walvis won election; seriously?

Reading Zone 5

1. According to the passage, proprietary restaurants in Las Vegas are
   (E) creative and individual

2. The phrase "put on the dog," as used in the passage, means
   (B) become more fancy

3. According to the author, casino restaurants have an advantage over independent restaurants because
   (B) their operations are subsidized by gambling revenues

4. According to the author, food in Las Vegas can be generally described as
   (D) competitive and differentiated

5. According to the passage, the gourmet rooms
   (D) are staffed by some of the best chefs in the country

6. An adjective used in the passage to describe the overall diversity and quality of the dining experience in Las Vegas is
   (E) respectable

7. The Las Vegas term "gourmet room" means
   (E) a designer restaurant

8. According to the author, dining in Las Vegas would be less palatable without
   (B) the increase in foreign visitors

9. What does the author mean by a "proprietary restaurant"?
   (A) Privately owned

10. Which of the following, if true, would most undermine the author's experience of dining in Las Vegas?
    (D) Las Vegas charges a minimum food tax of 73%.

Chapter 6

Exercise 6.1

1. a lock and key
2. a hemisphere
3. the Arctic
4. an atlas
5. kleptomania
6. an assembly line
7. friction
8. a pencil
9. vocal cords
10. Elvis Presley

Exercise 6.2

1. reaction + heat = good; reaction + HEAT = bad; reaction + catalyst = great

2. Nichiren = patriotic Buddhism → revival in S. G. movement

3.

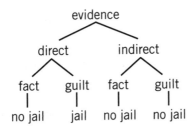

4.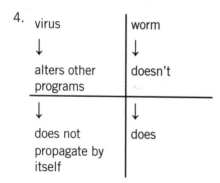

virus	worm
↓	↓
alters other programs	doesn't
↓	↓
does not propagate by itself	does

5. (Tax Reporter)
ACRS

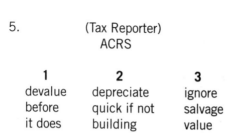

1	**2**	**3**
devalue	depreciate	ignore
before	quick if not	salvage
it does	building	value

Reading Zone 6

1. The main question addressed by the passage is
   (E) What is energy?

2. Conservation of energy, as described in the passage, is exhibited in
   (A) two ball bearings colliding

3. Conservation of mass is mentioned in the passage because
   (D) it is a concept in chemistry that is similar to the conservation of energy in physics

4. If a car were to slam into a large mound of wet clay, a probable result would be
   (E) a rise in clay temperature

5. In the passage, the term "elastic" means
   (D) hard and springy

Chapter 7

Exercise 7

Title	Helpful?
1. Financial Accounting for Beginners	No
2. Vietnam: The Untold Story of Government Corruption	Yes
3. From Fish to Man: Evolution's Progress	Yes
4. Russia's Quiet Threat	Yes
5. America the Beautiful	Yes
6. Society and Social Structures	No
7. Myths of Gender	Yes
8. Why I Kill: A Psychological Study	Yes
9. Parents and Children: The Communication Gap	Yes
10. The Evolution of Nuclear Strategy	No
11. Zen and the Art of Motorcycle Maintenance	Yes
12. Advanced Pascal	No
13. On Becoming a Novelist	No
14. Reading Smart	No
15. Information, Incentives, and Bargaining in the Japanese Economy	No

Reading Zone 7

1. Cornelius de Houtman could be described as
   (D) an ineffective commandant

2. The Dutch East India Company at first encountered
   (B) limited success

3. The Dutch control of the spice trade in Java was achieved through
   (C) sordid alliances

4. During the siege of Coen's position, his soldiers behaved
   (D) with dipsomaniac fervor

5. It can be inferred from the passage that the word "farang" means
   (B) foreigners

Chapter 8

Card 8.2

Postmodernism is an attitude we have now; it affects how we hear music from different times.

Card 8.3

Hegel had a modern idea of "dialectic" that was kind of different from Kant and that had something to do with all things being connected.

Card 8.4

Beckett is super bleak about humanity, but really interesting.

Reading Zone 8

1. From 1895 to 1903, Gauguin's artistic activity can best be described as
   (D) frenzied

2. It can be inferred from the passage that the word "oeuvre" means
   (B) area of obsession

3. Which of the following statements is best supported by the passage?
(D) Paul Gauguin was not confined to one area of expression.

4. Paul Gauguin's later work was
(D) informed by philosophical issues

5. Gauguin's exhibition of 1893 was marked by
(A) scenes from daily life

Chapter 9

Reading Zone 9

1. According to the passage, the word "hamlet" could best be defined as:
(D) a small town

2. The tone of the passage can best be described as primarily
(A) journalistic

3. The best description of Holcomb before the shotgun blasts would be
(A) homogeneous and peaceful

4. The violence of the shotgun blasts seemed, to the author, to be
(C) a shocking occurrence, forever changing this otherwise peaceful town

5. It can be inferred from the passage that the people killed by the shotgun blasts were
(D) residents of the town

Chapter 10

Exercise 10

1. plot
2. character
3. character
4. character
5. character

6. character
7. character
8. character
9. setting

Reading Zone 10

1. The relationship between Norton and Sheppard can best be described as
   (C) uncommunicative and disjointed

2. According to Sheppard, operating a small loan company would be
   (C) a fate similar to losing one's soul

3. How does the author intend the reader to interpret Sheppard's name?
   (A) Ironically

4. Why does the author keep referring to the character as "the child" instead of "Norton"?
   (D) To establish distance between Norton and the reader

5. According to Sheppard, what's the least desirable fault someone can have?
   (B) Selfishness

Chapter 11

Reading Zone 11

1. Which of the following excerpts is not an opinion?
   (A) "[A] checkrein on Chinese behavior that has since vanished was the threat of the Soviet Union."

2. Which of the following quotations is a primary fact?
   (D) "The Chinese are using their new wealth to make themselves a big military power in the region."

3. Which sentence best summarizes the author's argument?
   (E) The dissolution of the Soviet Union has fundamentally changed the United States-Vietnam relationship.

4. According to the passage, all of the following contributes to the perceived power vacuum in East Asia EXCEPT
   (C) the Vietnamese disarmament along Cambodian borders

5. According to the author, which of the following is the primary reason behind Vietnam's attempt to make peace with the United States?
   (B) The looming threat of China

6. America's financial relationship with the East is
   (D) all of the above

7. According to the passage, in the face of global demilitarization, China is
   (D) rearming with modern weaponry

8. The author's main reason for why the United States must "play the role of regional balancer" is inherently
   (A) economic

9. We can infer from the passage that since 1979 Vietnam's relationship with China has been
(B) degenerating

10. What, according to the passage, would the United States gain from an open relationship with Vietnam?
(D) A military presence in the Far East

Exercise 11.2

1. At the time this article was written, was the mayor of Chicago a Democrat or a Republican?
Democrat

2. According to the article, which party was most likely to hold their convention first in 1996?
Republican

3. Give two reasons the Democrats considered holding their convention in Chicago.

   • The DNC chairman lives in Chicago and advises the mayor.

   • Mayor Daley's brother William helped Clinton pass the North American Free Trade Agreement.

4. Give two reasons the Republicans considered holding their convention in Chicago.

   Possible answers:
   • The Governor of Illinois was a Republican.

   • Chicago has historical significance for the Republicans (14 Republican conventions have been held there.)

   • Illinois was a key state in the 1996 Presidential race.

5. What was the relationship between the mayor of Chicago and the governor of Illinois at the time this article was written?
cooperative

6. Why would Chicago have wanted to host either convention?
money

7. What factors worked against Chicago holding either convention?
the fiasco of the 1968 Democratic Convention

Chapter 12

Exercise 12

This is one (brief) analysis of "Words," written by Sylvia Plath in 1963, right before her death. Does knowing this fact make you want to reread the poem in light of it?

Words are important and powerful ("Axes/After whose stroke the wood rings"), free and indeterminate ("traveling/Off from the center like horses"), but fate ("fixed stars") triumphs over mere words in the end. Yet words write the poem. They guide us to the "fixed star" of fate.

Chapter 13

Reading Zone 13.1

1. What profession does the author of the passage liken to being a good writer?
(D) Doctor

2. Which of the following adjectives does the author use to characterize the profession of writing?
(B) Solitary

3. A book written by the author of the passage is called
(E) *The Love Letters*

4. As defined in the passage, a "trade novel" is
(E) one marketed for a general audience

5. According to the passage, all of the following are things the author explains to her creative writing classes EXCEPT
(D) resonance

6. The author has had to resist the label of being a(n)
(A) children's author

7. The author would most likely DISAGREE with which of the following statements?
(D) Difficult concepts should be written about with adults in mind, not children.

8. Her annotation of the contract selling her rights, excluding those rights in Sagittarius and the Andromeda Galaxy, was meant to be
(B) ironic

9. For whom does the author write?
(A) The work

10. Which of the following summarizes the main point of the passage?
(B) Whereas certain types of writers write for an audience, the fiction writer should write for the work.

Reading Zone 13.2

1. The characters in the passage are concerned with what natural phenomenon?
(B) Drought

2. An image that appears throughout the passage is
(E) all of the above

3. The tone of the passage is
(D) biblical

4. The attitude of the passage is
(B) pessimistic

5. The image of the men in the doorway at the end is most likely meant to inspire
(B) despair

6. The phrase "[t]he dawn came but no day" means that
(B) the sun rose but no light could be seen

7. This passage would be most appropriate as
(A) the opening to a novel

8. Which of the following is given human attributes throughout the passage?
(E) All of the above

9. The term "rainheads" as used in the passage means
(D) light sprinkling

10. The dust settling like "pollen" in the houses is meant to be
(A) a painful and ironic reminder of the land's infertility

Reading Zone 13.3

1. According to the passage, the picture of Kim Il Sung as an uninvolved, relaxed man is
(C) difficult to believe

2. The annual military exercise between South Korea and the United States was known as
(E) the Team Spirit

3. According to the passage, all of the following are attributed to the North Koreans EXCEPT
(B) raiding the South Korean border for supplies

4. According to the passage, the economic state of affairs in North Korea is considered
(A) dire

5. Kim Il Sung's attitude toward war can best be described as
(B) brinksmanship

6. The author would most likely DISAGREE with which of the following statements?
(C) The on-site nuclear inspections will most likely, under the I.A.E.A., go smoothly.

7. The North Koreans despise the Americans because of
(C) resentment over the splitting of Korea after World War II

8. As described in the passage, the term "journalistic chest" means
(D) investigative prize

9. The tone of the passage can best be described as
(D) warning

10. According to the passage, tours to North Korea can be best described as
(D) limited and unrevealing

Reading Zone 13.4

1. How does the passage characterize Hellenistic culture?
(B) Cosmopolitan and urbane

2. All of the following are characteristic of Hellenistic culture EXCEPT
(A) a lesser emphasis on man

3. Who wrote the *Argonautica*?
(D) Apollonius

4. According to the passage, all of the following were achievements of Archimedes EXCEPT
   (B) advances in geometry

5. One of the famous libraries of the Greek civilization was located in
   (E) Antioch

6. According to the passage, Greek culture spread to all of the following places EXCEPT
   (B) the Middle East

7. Who wrote the *Histories*?
   (A) Polybius

8. According to the passage, which best describes the development of knowledge in the Hellenistic era?
   (B) More specialized

9. Which of the following in use today were developed during the Hellenistic era?
   (D) All of the above

10. All of the following were Hellenistic figures EXCEPT
    (C) Aristotle

Reading Zone 13.5

1. Who says "you couldn't feel safe anywhere, except in the desert perhaps"?
   (D) The hostess

2. What is the narrator's tone?
   (A) Ironic

3. When would be the appropriate era for this piece?
   (B) World War II

4. What was a subject of discussion prior to dinner?
   (B) The octogenarian's condition

5. Why did the football player accuse the narrator of being a traitor?
   (D) The narrator remained silent.

6. To whom did the octogenarian tell the story of his accident?
   (E) No one at all

7. According to the passage, the hostess has never traveled to
   (C) Germany

8. What topic "stimulated the adrenal glands" of one of the guests?
   (C) The main course

9. How long had the author been in Hollywood on the evening discussed?
   (B) He was spending his first night in Hollywood.

10. Which of the following best describes the author's attitude toward the other guests?
    (C) Dislike

Grateful acknowledgment is made to the following for permission to reprint previously published material:

Excerpt from *The Washington Post,* February 27th © 2016 The Washington Post. All rights reserved. Used by permission and protected by the Copyright Laws of the United States. The printing, copying, redistribution, or retransmission of this Content without express written permission is prohibited.

Excerpt from marthagraham.org/about-us/our-history. Reprinted with permission of the Martha Graham Dance Company. © 2016.

Excerpt from *Postmodern Music/Postmodern Thought* by Judith Irene Lochhead and Joseph Henry Auner, eds. Reproduced with permission of Routledge via Copyright Clearance Center.

Excerpt from "Theories of Media" by Kim O'Connor, http://csmt.uchicago.edu/glossary2004/dialectic.htm. Reprinted with permission of the University of Chicago.

"Chapter 1," from *The Grapes of Wrath: 75th Anniversary Edition* by John Steinbeck, copyright 1939, renewed © 1967 by John Steinbeck. Used by permission of Viking Books, an imprint of Penguin Publishing Group, a division of Penguin Random House LLC.

Excerpt from *Forbes,* January 31, 1994 © 1994 Forbes. All rights reserved. Used by permission and protected by the Copyright Laws of the United States. The printing, copying, redistribution, or retransmission of this Content without express written permission is prohibited.

"Soirée in Hollywood" by Henry Miller, from *The Air-Conditioned Nightmare,* copyright © 1945 by New Directions Publishing Corp. Reprinted by permission of New Directions Publishing Corp.

Notes

Notes

The
Princeton
Review®

International Offices Listing

China (Beijing)
1501 Building A,
Disanji Creative Zone,
No.66 West Section of North 4th Ring Road Beijing
Tel: +86-10-62684481/2/3
Email: tprkor01@chol.com
Website: www.tprbeijing.com

China (Shanghai)
1010 Kaixuan Road
Building B, 5/F
Changning District, Shanghai, China 200052
Sara Beattie, Owner: Email: sbeattie@sarabeattie.com
Tel: +86-21-5108-2798
Fax: +86-21-6386-1039
Website: www.princetonreviewshanghai.com

Hong Kong
5th Floor, Yardley Commercial Building
1-6 Connaught Road West, Sheung Wan, Hong Kong
(MTR Exit C)
Sara Beattie, Owner: Email: sbeattie@sarabeattie.com
Tel: +852-2507-9380
Fax: +852-2827-4630
Website: www.princetonreviewhk.com

India (Mumbai)
Score Plus Academy
Office No.15, Fifth Floor
Manek Mahal 90
Veer Nariman Road
Next to Hotel Ambassador
Churchgate, Mumbai 400020
Maharashtra, India
Ritu Kalwani: Email: director@score-plus.com
Tel: + 91 22 22846801 / 39 / 41
Website: www.score-plus.com

India (New Delhi)
South Extension
K-16, Upper Ground Floor
South Extension Part–1,
New Delhi-110049
Aradhana Mahna: aradhana@manyagroup.com
Monisha Banerjee: monisha@manyagroup.com
Ruchi Tomar: ruchi.tomar@manyagroup.com
Rishi Josan: Rishi.josan@manyagroup.com
Vishal Goswamy: vishal.goswamy@manyagroup.com
Tel: +91-11-64501603/ 4, +91-11-65028379
Website: www.manyagroup.com

Lebanon
463 Bliss Street
AlFarra Building - 2nd floor
Ras Beirut
Beirut, Lebanon
Hassan Coudsi: Email: hassan.coudsi@review.com
Tel: +961-1-367-688
Website: www.princetonreviewlebanon.com

Korea
945-25 Young Shin Building
25 Daechi-Dong, Kangnam-gu
Seoul, Korea 135-280
Yong-Hoon Lee: Email: TPRKor01@chollian.net
In-Woo Kim: Email: iwkim@tpr.co.kr
Tel: + 82-2-554-7762
Fax: +82-2-453-9466
Website: www.tpr.co.kr

Kuwait
ScorePlus Learning Center
Salmiyah Block 3, Street 2 Building 14
Post Box: 559, Zip 1306, Safat, Kuwait
Email: infokuwait@score-plus.com
Tel: +965-25-75-48-02 / 8
Fax: +965-25-75-46-02
Website: www.scorepluseducation.com

Malaysia
Sara Beattie MDC Sdn Bhd
Suites 18E & 18F
18th Floor
Gurney Tower, Persiaran Gurney
Penang, Malaysia
Email: tprkl.my@sarabeattie.com
Sara Beattie, Owner: Email: sbeattie@sarabeattie.com
Tel: +604-2104 333
Fax: +604-2104 330
Website: www.princetonreviewKL.com

Mexico
TPR México
Guanajuato No. 242 Piso 1 Interior 1
Col. Roma Norte
México D.F., C.P.06700
registro@princetonreviewmexico.com
Tel: +52-55-5255-4495
+52-55-5255-4440
+52-55-5255-4442
Website: www.princetonreviewmexico.com

Qatar
Score Plus
Office No: 1A, Al Kuwari (Damas)
Building near Merweb Hotel, Al Saad
Post Box: 2408, Doha, Qatar
Email: infoqatar@score-plus.com
Tel: +974 44 36 8580, +974 526 5032
Fax: +974 44 13 1995
Website: www.scorepluseducation.com

Taiwan
The Princeton Review Taiwan
2F, 169 Zhong Xiao East Road, Section 4
Taipei, Taiwan 10690
Lisa Bartle (Owner): lbartle@princetonreview.com.tw
Tel: +886-2-2751-1293
Fax: +886-2-2776-3201
Website: www.PrincetonReview.com.tw

Thailand
The Princeton Review Thailand
Sathorn Nakorn Tower, 28th floor
100 North Sathorn Road
Bangkok, Thailand 10500
Thavida Bijayendrayodhin (Chairman)
Email: thavida@princetonreviewthailand.com
Mitsara Bijayendrayodhin (Managing Director)
Email: mitsara@princetonreviewthailand.com
Tel: +662-636-6770
Fax: +662-636-6776
Website: www.princetonreviewthailand.com

Turkey
Yeni Sülün Sokak No. 28
Levent, Istanbul, 34330, Turkey
Nuri Ozgur: nuri@tprturkey.com
Rona Ozgur: rona@tprturkey.com
Iren Ozgur: iren@tprturkey.com
Tel: +90-212-324-4747
Fax: +90-212-324-3347
Website: www.tprturkey.com

UAE
Emirates Score Plus
Office No: 506, Fifth Floor
Sultan Business Center
Near Lamcy Plaza, 21 Oud Metha Road
Post Box: 44098, Dubai
United Arab Emirates
Hukumat Kalwani: skoreplus@gmail.com
Ritu Kalwani: director@score-plus.com
Email: info@score-plus.com
Tel: +971-4-334-0004
Fax: +971-4-334-0222
Website: www.princetonreviewuae.com

Our International Partners

The Princeton Review also runs courses with a variety of
partners in Africa, Asia, Europe, and South America.

Georgia
LEAF American-Georgian Education Center
www.leaf.ge

Mongolia
English Academy of Mongolia
www.nyescm.org

Nigeria
The Know Place
www.knowplace.com.ng

Panama
Academia Interamericana de Panama
http://aip.edu.pa/

Switzerland
Institut Le Rosey
http://www.rosey.ch/

All other inquiries, please email us at
internationalsupport@review.com